DATE DUE

Nov 11 65			
Jan 4 '67			
GAYLORD			PRINTED IN U.S.A

THE BOURGEOIS POET

BY *Karl Shapiro*

THE
BOURGEOIS
POET

Karl Shapiro

RANDOM HOUSE NEW YORK

SECOND PRINTING

Library of Congress Catalog Card Number: 64-10356

MANUFACTURED IN THE UNITED STATES OF AMERICA BY
THE HADDON CRAFTSMEN INC., SCRANTON, PA.

DESIGN BY *Tere LoPrete*

How many precautions are necessary to keep oneself from lying!

*

That frightful quantity of I's and me's!

*

What! Is it nothing but that?

                    The Life of Henri Brulard

I
The Bourgeois Poet

❡ 1

The world is my dream, says the wise child, ever so wise, not stepping on lines. I am the world, says the wise-eyed child. I made you, mother. I made you, sky. Take care or I'll put you back in my dream.

If I look at the sun the sun will explode, says the wicked boy. If I look at the moon I'll drain away. Where I stay I hold them in their places. Don't ask me what I'm doing.

The simple son was sent to science college. There he learned how everything worked.

The one who says nothing is told everything (not that he cares). The one who dreamed me hasn't put me back.

The sun and the moon, they rise on time. I still don't know how the engine works; I can splice a wire. That's about it.

The dream is my world, says the sick child. I am pure as these bed sheets. (He writes fatigue on the vast expanses.) I'm in your dream, says the wicked boy. The simple son has been decorated for objectivity. He who says nothing is still being told.

De Sade looks down through the bars of the Bastille. They have stepped up the slaughter of nobles.

(2

The look of shock on an old friend's face after years of not meeting, as if perhaps we were in a play, dressed for one of the final acts. The make-up of the years (infant, schoolboy, lover, soldier, judge of others, patriarch and ultimate old child) is on us. Those who remain the same and those who change their jaws. One has milky moons around the eyes or knotty knuckles. Many and varied are the studies in gray. The spectrum of whites amazes.

A generation moves in stateliness. It arrives like a pageant and passes down the street. The children sit on the curbs and watch. There are dignitaries and clowns, the men with medals and the cross-carriers. The owners walk abreast for the afternoon: they carry the banner which reads: the business of the world is—business. Manacled dictators walk alone through the crowded silence: four swordsmen guard them like points of the compass. The poets arrive on burros, bumping each other. Theologians packed in a hearse peer out like sickly popes. A phalanx of technologists singing the latest love songs in marching rhythms. Movie stars escorting diplomats (it's hard to tell them apart).

Nine of the greatest novelists, of ridiculous difference in height and girth. Two modern saints on litters. The generation proceeds to the cenotaph, the only common meeting place. In side streets the coming generation, not even looking, waits its turn and practices a new and secret language. (They think it's secret: that's what's so depressing.) Their hero is also gray and still in high school. He drives a hundred miles an hour into a tree.

⟆3

Oriental, you give and give. No Christian ever gave like you. What is it you are giving morning and night, asking nothing in return? Pearls, silk cloths, books and scrolls, mother-of-pearl chopsticks, bronze cowbells, hand-painted poetry, tributes of every description. Flowers around my neck, morning, noon, and night: I am ready to vomit. You lay all Asia at my feet—where is your modern sense of values? You're not like a Frenchman, who gives as an investment. Not like an American whose gifts fall out of his pocket. Your gifts are permanent, an end in themselves. We'll cure you yet.

A rope of jasmine flowers round my neck at the airport, the the embarrassing bow, the immaculate dark men come with their cargo. The frenzied Westerner grabs it all, the powder barrel stowed under the high altar, in case. The wise men continue to give: a sack of spices for the rotten meat of English queens; antimacassars; Zen.

It's as if you said, that's all I have to give, namely, the works. You never say, leave us alone. That's Western talk. You say, come for a swim in the old sky: my eyes are upside down. You say, the turtle can draw in its legs; the seer can draw in his senses; I call him illumined. In India eyes are never wide open. I throw a bucket of cold water over your continent. Get up from your bed of nails, you wise men of the East. I'm giving you a power plant for Christmas.

¶4

The rice around the lingam stone will be distributed in the dying sun to the unblessed poor. I bring neither rice nor overpowering jasmine but only my full gaze of love and loathing. With the beautiful Hindu woman I drink in the phallus. On her face the trace of a sneer. (She may be Christian.) Under the nine domes of the Kali temple we make our way to the Divine Mother, Savior of the Universe, Kali in basalt, in gold and precious stones. She stands on Siva. A garland of skulls hangs from her neck. In one of her four hands a severed human head; with another she gives the sign of peace. Her triple eyes bring peace or terror. This was Rama-krishna's darling, standing on Siva, who lies supine on the thousand-petaled silver-lotus.

He drank her smile till all was blue, that saint. He joined the
hands of all the gods. In his room a picture of Christ
as well. He reached the seventh plane at will.

¶5

Of love and death in the Garrison State I sing. From uni-
formed populations rises the High Art, *Oedipus King*,
the Nō, the ballerina bleeding in her slippers. At the
Officer's Club adultery is rationed (their children are
not allowed to play with guns; this helps whet their
appetite). The ladies are discussing the chemical control of behavior by radio waves: that will solve the
problem of neighbors. Symposia on causes of desertion
draw record-breaking crowds. The handsomer pacifists
are invited to the most sought-after cocktail parties.
The women try their hand at them in the rumpus room;
some progress reported. Waves of asceticism sweep the
automobile industry. The mere sight of a Sam Browne
belt, which used to inspire contempt, brings tears to
the eyes of high-school boys. All flabby citizens are
automatically put under surveillance. Chess problems
supersede crap in the noncoms' barracks. The sacred
number is Two: two parties, two powers sworn to
mutual death, two poles of everything from ethics to
magnetics. It's a balanced society.

Today the order goes out: all distant places are to be abol-
ished: beachcombers are shot like looters. Established
poets are forced to wear beards and bluejeans; they are
treated kindly in bohemian zoos; mysterious stipends
drift their way. They can trade soap for peyote at

specified libraries. Children's prizes are given for essays on the pleasures of crisis. Historians are awarded all the key posts in the foreign office. Sculptors who use old shrapnel are made the heads of schools of design. Highways move underground like veins of ore. The Anti-Sky Association (volunteer contributions only) meets naked at high noon and prays for color blindness.

"Color is a biological luxury."

¶6

Quintana lay in the shallow grave of coral. The guns boomed stupidly fifty yards away. The plasma trickled into his arm. Naked and filthy, covered with mosquitoes, he looked at me as I read his white cloth tag. How do you feel, Quintana? He looks away from my gaze. I lie: we'll get you out of here sometime today.

I never saw him again, dead or alive. Skin and bones, with eyes as soft as soot, neck long as a thigh, a cross on his breastbone not far from the dog tags. El Greco was all I could think of. Quintana lying in his shallow foxhole waiting to be evacuated. A dying man with a Spanish name equals El Greco. A truck driver from Dallas probably.

When the Japs were making the banzai charge, to add insult to death, they came at us screaming the supreme insult: *Babe Ruth, go to hell!* The Americans, on the other hand, when the Japs flew over dropping sticks of explosives, shouted into the air, as if they could hear: *Tojo eat shit!*

Soldiers fall in love with the enemy all too easily. It's the allies they hate. Every war is its own excuse. That's why they're all surrounded with ideals. That's why they're all crusades.

¶7

The bourgeois poet closes the door of his study and lights his pipe. Why am I in this box, he says to himself (although it is exactly as he planned). The bourgeois poet sits down at his inoffensive desk—a door with legs, a door turned table—and almost approves the careful disarray of books, papers, magazines and such artifacts as thumbtacks. The bourgeois poet is already out of matches and gets up. It is too early in the morning for any definite emotion and the B.P. smokes. It is beautiful in the midlands: green fields and tawny fields, sorghum the color of red morocco bindings, distant new neighborhoods, cleanly and treeless, and the Veterans Hospital fronted with a shimmering Indian Summer tree. The Beep feels seasonal, placid as a melon, neat as a child's football lying under the tree, waiting for whose hands to pick it up.

¶8

Office love, love of money and fight, love of calculated sex. The offices reek with thin volcanic metal. Tears fall in typewriters like drops of solder. Brimstone of brassieres, low voices, the whirr of dead-serious play. From the tropical tree and the Rothko in the Board Room to the ungrammatical broom closet fragrant with waxes, to the vast typing pool where coffee is being served by dainty waitresses maneuvering their hand trucks, music almost unnoticeable falls. The very telephones are hard and kissable, the electric water cooler sweetly sweats. Gold simmers to a boil in braceleted and sunburned cheeks. What ritual politeness nevertheless, what subtlety of clothing. And if glances meet, if shoulders graze, there's no harm done. Flowers, celebrations, pregnancy leave, how the little diamonds sparkle under the psychologically soft-colored ceilings. It's an elegant windowless world of soft pressures and efficiency joys, of civilized mishaps—mere runs in the stocking, papercuts.

Where the big boys sit the language is rougher. Phone calls to China and a private shower. No paper visible anywhere. Policy is decided by word of mouth like gangsters. There the power lies and is sexless.

¶9

Lower the standard: that's my motto. Somebody is always putting the food out of reach. We're tired of falling off ladders. Who says a child can't paint? A pro is somebody who does it for money. Lower the standards. Let's all play poetry. Down with ideals, flags, convention buttons, morals, the scrambled eggs on the admiral's hat. I'm talking sense. Lower the standards. Sabotage the stylistic approach. Let weeds grow in the subdivi-

sion. Putty up the incisions in the library façade, those
names that frighten grade-school teachers, those names
whose U's are cut like V's. Burn the *Syntopicon* and
The Harvard Classics. Lower the standard on classics,
battleships, Russian ballet, national anthems (but
they're low enough). Break through to the bottom. Be
natural as an American abroad who knows no language,
not even American. Keelhaul the poets in the vestry
chairs. Renovate the Abbey of cold-storage dreamers.
Get off the Culture Wagon. Learn how to walk the way
you want. Slump your shoulders, stick your belly out,
arms all over the table. How many generations will this
take? Don't think about it, just make a start. (You have
made a start.) Don't break anything you can step
around, *but don't pick it up*. The law of gravity is the
law of art. You first, poetry second, the good, the beautiful, the true come last. As the lad said: We must love
one another or die.

¶ 10

Waiting in front of the columnar high school (the old ones
look like banks, or rather insurance companies) I
glance over the top of my book. The bells go off like
slow burglar alarms; innumerable sixteeners saunter
out. There's no running as in the lower schools, none
of that helpless gaiety of the small. Here comes a surly
defiance. As in a ritual, each lights a cigaret just at the
boundary where the tabu ends. Each chews. The ones
in cars rev up their motors and have bad complexions
like gangsters. The sixteeners are all playing gangster.

The sea of subjectivity comes at you like a tidal wave, splashing the cuffs of middle-aged monuments. War is written on their unwritten faces. They try out wet dreams and wandering mind. They're rubbing Aladdin's lamp in the locker room. They pray for moments of objectivity as drunkards pray for the one that puts you out. They've captured the telephone centers, the microphones, the magazine syndicates (they've left the movies to us). I wait behind the wheel and spy; it's enemy territory all right. My daughter comes, grows taller as she approaches. It's a moment of panic.

But once at night in the sweet and sour fall I dropped her off at the football game. The bowl of light lit up the creamy Corinthian columns. A cheer went up from the field so shrill, so young, like a thousand birds in a single cage, like a massacre of child-brides in a clearing, I felt ashamed and grave. The horror of their years stoned me to death.

¶ 1 1

The cat, outrageously unprepared for life, delicately kicking over everything he passes, creating virtual disasters, a too-excellent judge of human personality, impartial to a fault, comatose usually but never really, a vegetable version of his larger uncles, an indifferent mouser, conscienceless thing that can't distinguish between work and play. No house should be without this abdicator. (One has the feeling it dethroned itself.)

The cat, with patronizing ways, eats practically nothing, then if it can get one, will hog a whole rabbit or lug it into the house, alive, torn open, and lay it at your feet, as it were. It cleans itself like a woman trying on gloves. It chews out loud like a peasant. It responds to sensuality not to kindness, as we generally suppose.

Its sexual proclivities have been discussed elsewhere. A battle-scarred tom, whole pelts removed, looks like a movie-star marine. The eunuch cat is massive, Buddhistic, splendidly immobile, apparently above even castration. The young cat skitters at its shadow, developing fears so disproportionate to any event that one is tempted to make it purr. The purr is really a wakeful snore, about as personal as the humming of a telegraph wire. At bird-watching he is superbly criminal: after eons of observation, or it may be minutes, he kneads his fore-paws, waggles his butt and has what he wants. What's frightening is the lashing of the tail, like an amateur symphony conductor. The tip of the tail is telepathic, or seismographic. It registers nearness.

¶ 12

The dermatologist committed suicide, a good man, a sad man, with the hangdog mien of a proctologist.

Skin-watching, tricksy as palmistry, what medieval blips and scars, what outcroppings of thought! Maps of remorse, tattoos from voyages never undertaken, blueprints of literary cleverness, bad dreams of personal acid—the skin has wiles undreamed of by bacteria. Under the living continent of skin flows molten lava; heat spots and sinkings form, then violent eruption, appearance of crystals, the terrifying symmetry of disease. Thus the humiliation of itch- and scratch-lust, tearing of pleasure into pain, revenge of self and desecration of love.

So lay the mother of grown children, after the final consent to herself that the marriage was ended. The dermatologist pronounces the name of the rare sickness. She will lose her skin from top to toe, fingernails, toenails. Yet she will be like new, without a scar, made perfect after agony.

(13

Italy spoiled California for me. California spoiled Italy. Now I'm back in the Middle West, where I don't really belong. Nor can I go back East. Living in that Etruscan pine forest, maddened by too much sun, I watched the clouds gather up where Siena would be, and no rain came. Admittedly, it was the drying season. Heat of Florence on a Sunday afternoon. The horse almost fainted, pulling six in a buggy. Floods at Christmas in the Sacramento Valley: camellias floating in the gutters. The final fakery of palm trees in the palm-tree countries: emblem of grandiose injustice. In Nebraska the Russian olive, fruitless. Drunken smell of pine between Fredericksburg and Richmond and atop the Donner Pass. In Italy the scent barely perceptible, the bland Mediterranean, reddish yolks of eggs and dirty shells. The large soft Californians sideswiping the future: the small burning Italians endlessly plotting nothing. Everywhere the competition of boasting. Only the Navajo questioning time: what is a year? he asks.

Does it have arms and legs? In Baltimore, walking in Victorian-movie snow it occurred to me: seek for the opposite. I'm for the Faustian supermarket. The opposite enthralls me. I refuse the wine of the locale. I smash customs like crockery. The Minnesota accent is music to my ears. The New Yorker is talking to me at top speed; the Frenchwoman flies into the conversation at breakneck; I slow them down with extreme modesty. Always at heart a central Californian, I nurse my own geography, miles of tomatoes, tons of sugar beets. I call a farm a ranch. But no palm trees.

¶14

The password of the twentieth century: Communications (as if we had to invent them). Animals and cannibals have communications; birds and bees and even a few human creatures, called artists (generally held to be insane). But the bulk of humanity had to invent Communications. The Romans had the best roads in the world, but had nothing to communicate over them except other Romans. Americans have conquered world-time and world-space and chat with the four corners of the earth at breakfast and have nothing to communicate except other Americans. The Russians communicate other Russians to the moon. The entire solar system is in the hands of cartoonists.

I am sitting in the kitchen in Nebraska and watching a shrouded woman amble down the market in Karachi. She is going to get her morning smallpox shot. It's cold and mental love they want: It's the mystic sexuality of Communications. Money was love. Power was love. Communications now are love. Sex-object of the telephone, let's kiss. The girl hugs the hi-fi speaker to her belly: it pours into her openings like gravy. In the spring, Hitler arises. This is the time of trampling. My japanned birds in the radioactive snow are calling.

A man appears at the corner of the street; I prepare myself for hospitality. Man or angel, welcome! But I am afraid and double-lock the door. On the occasion of the death of a political party, I send an epitaph by Western Union. I didn't go to the funeral of poetry. I stayed home and watched it on television. Moon in the bottom of the Steuben glass, sun nesting in New Mexican deserts—the primitive Christian communicated with a dirty big toe. He drew a fish in the dust.

⟪15

It's lovely when one of them with a high jeweled hat and a crucifix the size of George Washington's hatchet gets caught in the act. We hug ourselves with happiness. We shrug when we hear that the alcoholic Jesuit is spending the winter in medical seclusion, that the rabbi is laying the Ladies Aid Society, the baldheaded Buddhist smuggling in machine guns. It's hard to hate them when they're so human. All the tales of Boccaccio wine us and dine us even on the deathbed, holier-than-thou. No matter how hard they try to rub it out, religion has love and kisses at the bottom. And because we know it has love at the bottom we follow the helmeted chaplain into battle. Onward, he yells, for God and country. Hurrah for Israel! Long live the Holy Roman

Empire! Three cheers for Schleswig-Holstein and
Carthage, Illinois! (That's where the Mormons got it
in the neck.) In truth, there are two religions and two
American flags, one for the rich and one for the poor.
But they look so much alike we forget which one we
are following. And after that there's church, the cosmos
divided into calendar days and calendar hours. And in
atheist nations the calendar of revolutions that failed.
All of them fail, the heroes turned out of their graves.
In the long run the only hope is for more human error
on the part of the holy. Their sin is our salvation.

¶16

Abraham Lincoln wore the chimney hat and the smoke poured
from the mills. Now we go nude in artificial summer.
The sari is woman's most beautiful dress, though senseless in the snow. When men show their legs the skirts
of women drop to the ankle. The longer the skirt the
more of the bosom. A superior primitivism lays bare
the nipples. But when in the entire history of man has
he invented a more dreary uniform than the business
suit? Here is the husk of the drone, unornamented,
gray, the final comedown. Congo chief, back to your
feathers!

Alas for the language of clothes, now written in code. We
dress with scientific care, not to offend. Potentates
were crushed by the weight of raiment. Though beauty
makes its way through rags, extreme simplicity is a
sign of power. Clothes are designed for the state of the
hair. Those who afford elaborate hair are dressed in the
ransom of princes. In prison and armies they first cut

off your hair. The German haircut fits the iron heel.
The king in curls wears tapestry. The barrister's wig
bedecks the anachronism.

Children in uniform insult Jesus in heaven. A woman's under-
silks smell fresh in the nostrils of God. Put flowers in
thy hair. Keep hair in your armpits like the Italian
women. Go naked in furs like Fraulein Else. You men,
wear Texas hats: that's all that's left of the sale. And
never mind the lilies of the field: the nuns dress well,
whatever their religion. Puttees for men with doubtful
calves. Nightgowns are nonsense. And don't forget the
accessories.

¶17

The child who is silent stands against his father, lovingly
looking up at him as if to say without a trace of defiance: I will speak when I have decided. He marches
around the table smiling intelligently, now and then
deigning to say something, perhaps "locomotive." It
is somewhat frightening, a kind of rebuff to grownups.
The doctors smile and shrug. If the parents are worried
they don't display it. It's only like living in the last
house at the edge of the subdivision. There's a bit of
farm left and a highway beyond: if someone should
rattle the back door in the night . . . There is a child
of two minds who says nothing and who is drinking it
all in. Obviously happy, very much loved, handsome
and straight, laughing and playing, withholding that
gift we all abuse. In that room is a tower of books with
their backs to us, eloquently quiet too. Man is a torrent
of language, even in death. But visitors use longer
words. The little philosopher goes about his business.

This is the town where the railroads ended, the wagon trains formed in the dry gray grass. It's this frontier of speech we are always crossing. The locomotive is ridiculously dying, lumbering off to the deep clay pits to settle among the mastodon bones. The piano is thinking of Mozart. On the very top, legs crossed, at ease, sits the blue-eyed boy who holds his peace.

⁋18

One of those idle autumn evenings on a street as harmless as an Eskimo Pie, the young ones chatter on the porch with their aunt, a woman of intelligence, as they say. Someone across the street has died some days ago. Once in a while a long wail of a female voice, as though from a quite distant bedroom. It is somber and full of dread, yet only a phrase, a Berlioz tune. We discuss it thoroughly, how it trespasses on the music of the street. And the aunt, taking the side of the young perhaps, would quieten such grief, cure it more quickly, have it get up and bathe and fill its lungs with air and look at the world, though different now, but still the only world.

Spoken too soon. Another week and her husband dies, a man of reputation, in excellent health. Something has drawn me to her porch again: the family is coming from the cemetery. They carry her from the car; her screams rip through the harmless street. Others are running from other cars. By the end of the day half of her face is turned in paralysis. For months her mouth lies in a twist—that grief that parodies a smile.

⟨19

Always another proverb that contradicts the first one. What
matters who said it or where it came from? What
difference does it make if it's contradicted? All truths
are paired contradictions, half-truths are absolutes.
But the proverbist knows nothing of the two sides of
a question. He knows only the roundness of answers.
The ball is followed by the child. Proverbs are what's
left of literature after the smoke has cleared away.
Proverbs wag their finger at the world. Proverbs always alliterate: that's one thing they have in common.
Proverbs are ads that have nothing to sell. Bibles are
loaded with proverbs.

Homely wisdom be damned. Let's get at the opposites. Even
conservatives believe in "two sides of the question." I
believe in four, eight, and ten sides to the question. The
answer is asymmetrical but whole. It's not as round as
a billiard ball. The world is not round. The sides of
your face are never alike. There's never been the same
face twice.

"Baroque is always *on the other hand*."

⟨20

Libraries, where one takes on the smell of books, stale and
attractive. Service with no motive, simple as U.S. Mail.
Fountains and palms, armchairs for smokers. Incred-
ible library where ideas run for safety, place of rebirth
of forgotten anthems, modern cathedral for lovers.

Library, hotel lobby for the unemployed, the failure, the boy afraid to go home, penniless. Switchboards for questioners: What do you know about unicorns? How do you address a duchess? Palladian architecture of gleaming glass and redwood. Window displays of this week's twelve best-sellers. Magnificent quarters of the director, who dines with names of unknown fame. Lavatories, rendezvous of desperate homosexuals. In the periodical room the newspapers bound with a stick, carried like banners of surrender to pale oak tables. Library, asylum, platform for uninhibited leaps. In the genealogy room the delicate perspiration of effete brains. Room also of the secret catalogue, room of un-listed books, those sought by police, manuscript room with the door of black steel, manuscripts stolen in delicate professional theft from abroad, sealed for seventy-five years. Sutras on spools of film. And all this courtesy and all this trust, tons of trash and tons of greatness, burning in time with the slow cool burning, burning in the fires of poems that gut libraries, only to rebuild them, more grand and Palladian, freer, more courteous, with cornerstones that say: Decide for your-self.

¶21

The two-year-old has had a motherless week. Mother has gone to bring back the baby. A week is many many years. One evening they bring the news to the playpen: a child is born, you have a baby brother. The dark little eyes consider this news and convey no message. One day long after, they arrive in a taxi, father, mother, bundle. The two-year-old observes from her blue walker on the sunny sidewalk. She stares and turns away on her wheels.

The father has gone to the other side of the world. He will bring back strange presents to a strange house. The little ones shyly wait their turn. Reconciliation is gradual.

In Trenton, New Jersey, the soldiers sit in the innocuous bar. It's three years since they saw the ones they wrote to. They are all afraid to go home. One lives two blocks away; he is very silent. Late in the afternoon, at an ungiven signal, they get up and disperse, like criminals perfectly trained for the job ahead.

In my brother's house when I left (whole histories ago) the furniture was honeymoon fresh, gleam of ceramics; soft beige carpets smelt like new-mown hay. With a shock I see the carpet is worn; the sofa has settled; books have changed places. A thousand days of words have passed.

Time is mostly absences, oceans generally at peace, and lives we love most often out of reach.

¶22

All tropic places smell of mold. A letter from Karachi smells of mold. A book I had in New Guinea twenty years ago smells of mold. Cities in India smell of mold and dung. After a while you begin to like it. The curry dishes in the fine Bombay restaurant add the dung flavor. In the villages dung patties plastered to the walls, the leaving of cows the only cooking fuel. The smell rubs into the blood.

Paris in the winter smells of wood smoke and fruit. Near the Gare St. Lazare in the freezing dusk the crowds pour slowly down the streets in every direction. A police van the size of a Pullman car goes at a walking pace. The gendarme keeps jumping down from the rear like a streetcar conductor in the old days. He is examining identity cards of pedestrians, especially the females. A girl comes swinging along, her pocketbook in rhythm with her behind. She is bareheaded and wears a raincoat. The gendarme examines her identity card. She is motioned into the paddy wagon.

Salzburg, the castle smells of snow and peat. Baltimore, old oaken bucket. Portsmouth, Virginia, roses and diesel oil. Dublin, coal dust, saccharine whiskey, bitter bodies. Damp gusts of Siena doorways. Warehouses of Papeete, acrid smell of copra, frangipani, salt water and mold. Smell of rotting water in Hollandia.

Unbreathable jungles, parks subtle and cool. Backstage the ballet dancers wipe their sweat; "the entire stage stinks like a stable." Sewer gas of beauty parlors. Electric smell of hair in rut. Talcum powder, earliest recollection. Rome, the armpit of the universe.

¶23

From the top floor of the Tulsa hotel I gaze at the night beauty of the cracking-plant. Candlelit city of small gas flames by the thousands, what a lovely anachronism dancing below like an adolescent's dream of the 1880's, the holy gas redeemed from Baudelaire's mustachioed curses. Elsewhere are the white lights of the age, but here, like a millionaire who frowns on electricity, the opulence of flame. Descending on Rome from the air at night, a similar beauty: the weak Italian bulbs like faulty rheostats yellowly outline the baroque curves of the Tiber, the semicircles of the monstrous Vatican, endless broken parabolas.

The cracking-plant is equally palatial. Those oil men in the silent elevator, like princes with their voices of natural volume, their soft hats and their name-drops (like balloons of words in the mouths of caricatures in political cartoons), men of many mansions. The doors of the room are mahogany. Through one which adjoins and is locked I hear the guttural laughter of undress, neither leisurely nor quick, indistinct wording, and all is silent but a woman's moan. Now it rises like the grip of pain; it is almost loud; it is certainly sincere, like the pent-up grief of deep relief; now it is round, now vibrant, now it is scaly as it grows. (Then it steps off into nothingness.)

I stand awed in my stocking-feet and move respectfully toward the window, as a man in an art gallery moves toward a more distant masterpiece to avoid the musical chatter of intruders. The cracking-plant sails on through the delicate Oklahoma night, flying the thousand hot flags of Laputa.

¶24

There's a Parthenon in Nashville large as life, the only perfect replica. Greeks resent it probably: it sits flat on the ground, like a plane crash reconstructed. It's not that famous derelict in space (blasted to bits by a Venetian general). It's not real marble but the brownish concrete has the rusty tinge of the Pentelikon. The brownish yellow came from the Potomac. The British Government cast these Elgin marbles.

Stepping from your car beneath the West Pediment, you fall back foot after foot. It crouches over you, a dark red turmoil, savage, barbaric—how can this be! Those columns like piano legs, prototype of Middle Western banks, and brazen doors the biggest in the world. Only in the Naos where the goddess is gone (she's never been found, like Eve) the pallid beauty dawns and spreads like cunningly concealed electric light. The beautiful goddess of ivory and gold, torn into shreds for dagger grips or crucifixes, has no single worshiper left on the face of the earth, it says at the close of the guidebook. It was her temple, then it was a church, then it was a mosque (even with minaret!). Now it's the temple of art. We buy it and sell it fifty times a day. It's the warehouse of the spirit, a faulty translation.

You, Morosini, dread doge of Venice, what was it like when you saw the Explosion? A direct hit if there ever was one! And the Turks thought Athena would protect their gunpowder.

¶25

Between the *Times* and *Partisan*, Sestos and Abydos of aspiring poets. Between the itch for popularity and the refined thirst for the avant-garde. Between the picture on the opening page and the quiet hieratic promotion. Between the happy handshake and the imperceptible nod of acceptance. Between the goose that lays the golden egg and the tailor who weaves the emperor's clothes. Then silence.

A book is just a version of a tree (name it!). A book goes places like a broker's boy. A book goes like a bum. It's harder to go down than up. There's a high conspiracy to keep you up. You battle to go down and lose. They drag you out with cheers for the loser. Defeat is impossible. Still you retain the habit of struggle. But it does no good. There's only one defense: betray thyself.

You find a modicum of peace. You sleep the sleep of the anonymous. The young die in a blaze of headlines. The old and evil grow still more old, more evil. The *Times* remains the *Times;* the *Partisan* remains with its crew of Southern girls, slicing the fat from literature with hairline knives. (What is removed drops horribly in the pail.) Read by the young and the other half-educated, original books, poems with no heredity or environment, prophecies without political content, gracile provincial bibles. At the bottom of the garbage lie the actual poems.

¶26

Hart Crane, though handicapped, did well with the burlesk: all but her belly buried in the floor. Magdalene? Perhaps. In Kansas City I pay my respects to the dying art. The theater is in ruins, the ticket-taker only half-conscious. Wine took him long ago. The carpet in the aisle is ripped; twice I snag my foot. The rank air smells of disinfectant. All seats are vacant except the first two rows. These are lit up as in a Rembrandt picture, the glowing center of the operation. I sit down inches from the drum. It lifts my hair each second it is smashed. The snare drum hisses and the block clicks. The cymbal crazes.

She's halfway through, already down to the sash that hangs like a silk muffler between her buttocks. She gyrates with an expert beat, more round than sharp. Small-breasted, her nipples glitter with stardust—some local ordinance. She is very pretty, not what you would expect, almost indifferently dancing her career. Cold flows from her steady limbs; stately she spreads her thighs for the climactic grind, when at the highest throw she slips her final string, holding one hand over the part like a live fig leaf, and flittering her fingers off —and we are there, and she is all but hairless.

Our faces light up with intelligence.

❨27

Why poetry small and cramped, why poetry starved and mean, thin-lipped and sunken-cheeked? Why these pams, these narrow-shouldered negatives? (The best we can say is that they're seed catalogs.) And why those staring eyes, so carefully fixed on the photographic plate? Why no lips at all but in their stead the practiced line of anger and the clamped jaw? Why always the darkening halo, so seemingly satanic? (The best we can say is that they are trying to mirror our lives. Do they know our lives? Can they read past the symbols of our trade?) Why so much attention to the printed page, why the cosmetology of font and rule, meters laid on like fingernail enamel? Why these lisping indentations, Spanish question marks upside down? Why the attractive packaging of stanza? Those cartons so pretty, shall I open them up? Why the un-American-activity of the sonnet? Why must grown people listen to rhyme? How much longer the polite applause, the tickle in the throat?

What will fatten you, skinny little book? What will put lead in your pencil? All of you dust-collecting seed catalogs, to the Goodwill you go, to the broad stench of the paper mill! Seed catalog, go pulp yourself!

Poems, flowers of language, if that's what you are, grow up in the air where books come true. And you, thin packet, let your seed fly, if you have any.

¶28

Broken bottles hard-set in cement, green glass, brown glass, wavy white and blue, they glitter down the street like distant peaks. I call it St. Mary's of the broken bottle necks. It's the black belt of the town and the old convent. The mossy wall surmounted with jags and hates of glass, hard-set in cement, ledges of rotten ice, yet feminine.

When the sun strikes these fragments like stained glass, what do the sisters feel who walk within these walls? Here are no pictured saints leaded together from the days of blood. Here are the ugly claws of chastity, the long fingernails of theological grief, the severed tendons, castrations for all these perpetually mourning virgins, those lovely Héloïses awakened by knives, deliciously composing love letters forever.

Who drank from these bottles, cracked them so carefully and fixed them in the brick?

In a fine Connecticut living room I saw a Calder once of broken bottles strung in an empty frame. The necks hung free, turning slightly on their slender wires.

¶29

The living rooms of my neighbors are like beauty parlors, like night-club powder rooms, like international airport first-class lounges. The bathrooms of my neighbors are like love nests—Dufy prints, black Kleenex, furry towels, toilets so highly bred they fill and fall without a sigh (why is there no bidet in so-clean America?). The kitchens of my neighbors are like cars: what gleaming dials, what toothy enamels, engines that click and purr, idling the hours away. The basements of my neighbors are like kitchens; you could eat off the floor. Look at the furnace, spotless as a breakfront, standing alone, prize piece, the god of the household.

But I'm no different. I arrange my books with a view to their appearance. Some highbrow titles are prominently displayed. The desk in my study is carefully littered; after some thought I hang a diploma on the wall only to take it down again. I sit at the window where I can be seen. What do my neighbors think of me—I hope they think of me. I fix the light to hit the books. I lean some rows one way, some rows another.

A man's house is his stage. Others walk on to play their bit parts. Now and again a soliloquy, a birth, an adultery.

The bars of my neighbors are various, ranging from none at all to the nearly professional, leather stools, automatic coolers, a naked painting, a spittoon for show.

The businessman, the air-force captain, the professor with tenure—it's a neighborhood with a sky.

❡30

It happens sometimes in the best of families that a poet is born to destroy the family. Which only strengthens the family a hundredfold. It happens also in the least of families. Blue blood is harder to erase than ink. Blue blood is ink. It's a magic circle, gules, four roses or, like a colophon or a cut tattoo. To work the bad blood out is the problem, just like working the good blood in. Pitch your tent on the master's lawn in the talented dawn: rhyme like a chain gang. Ahead lie doors more frightening than Poe.

And you, the sad sardonic Jew, how is it to sleep with the blond novel? Gifts that you poured like a jewelry merchant in her wholesale lap! The deep scar I forget just where on your face, rich voice like a man's fur collar. Yours was the harder job in the sweatshop of ideas. As we get better we lose our minds.

The magazines pile up and die. It's autumn in the street of publishers. Prizes blow down the street like wrapping

paper. Hoodlums are making up private languages
(but we're no longer infuriated). Wisdom brings back
the basic beliefs of eighteen. We've gotten nowhere,
only better. Maybe we've started a family of our own,
black blood and tics of the neck. Younger we told each
other how to write, slashing each other's faces like
wrists. Fame delivered a hurry message at dinner.
Everyone forgot his manners in the excitement. The
menu was published along with the speeches. There's
always room in the history books.

⁋31

After a war the boys play soldier with real weapons. This is
a real hand grenade, a pineapple. The killing stuff has
been removed but the pin remains to pull out and
push in. There is a clip to hang it from your belt. The
pineapple is a red-brown iron the color of—a pineapple, very heavy to hold, very heavy to throw, though
small. All the boys own a pineapple. The squares are
cut deep in the metal fruit. When it explodes, we
say, you have diced pineapple and dying men and a
hole in the ground.

The dummy rifles are dark-brown wood. Every part is round
and smooth. There is no metal, no trigger assembly.
The dummy muzzle comes to a rubber end like a
truncheon or a heavy walking stick. It is five feet tall
and too heavy for boys to hold out straight in the
standing position, but fine to hold prone or stand in
the corner of the bedroom.

The shallow helmet is rough to the feel, a greenish basin
with a cocky steel brim. Inside, the webbing is leather

to fit the skull and carry the shock. Mine has a handsome dent in the top, a round dent with a crease at the bottom. There is a delicate line of rust in the crease, a close call for somebody.

Today we play on the gray wooden battleship built on the grass for the sailors' drills. This must be the biggest toy in the world, a full-sized ship, a ship out of water, all above ground, without a keel. The Naval Base is always open to boys. The Naval Base is filled with flowered walks and neat straight lines and whitewashed curbs. The officers' houses are white and face the Bay. The wooden battleship is a school. It never rocks but runs up fluttering flags. The ship browses at peace among the flowers of the Naval Base. The Shore Police in their sentry boxes at the main entrance don't even notice us as we come and go. We are part of the game.

The shell-shocked newsman stomps down Granby Street, shouting commands and thumping his truncheon-stick on the ground. Nobody laughs at him; everyone says he is harmless. The fits of stomping and shouting commands come once or twice a day. Then he subsides in a truce with himself. When there are parades he stands at attention.

Leaving the troopship, men hacked at walls, slit mattresses, broke pipes, gouged at lounge-room ornamentation, middle-class British taste for luxury liners, made minor desecrations of the great gray leviathan. On this voyage of forty days and forty nights the Americans consumed a quarter of a million Coca-Colas, the sergeant says, and spits between his feet.

The General returns with the power of a god. His disgrace is a triumph. The world pours at his feet like a tide; it swirls through cities and engulfs skyscrapers. Men become frightened at their own frenzy. In Chicago the cheering and weeping are endemic, maniacal. The General is handsome, arrogant, and wrong. Such a General might be the President. He leaves his car to lay a wreath on a bridge across the poisonous Chicago River. He delivers his profile to rich and poor. In the war his communiqués always mentioned God. We hated him.

❨32

The History of Philosophy professor is a fashion plate of superiority. There's not a note in sight: the desk in front of him is a useless prop left over by some amateur company. His timing is as elegant as that of the Budapest String Quartet. Small, handsome, dressed with the quiet of a minor prince who made off with the money, he never lights a cigaret until the question period. And never superior to the questioner—you would have to be his wife to know when he is impatient. In war he wears a Navy uniform of very serious rank.

Now we have shot Zeno's arrow, with inexplicable excitement. We have made a choice between Parmenides and Heraclitus. Myself, I write a paper on Lord Herbert and Thomas Jefferson. Spring comes with Schopenhauer. Exams flush everything out of our minds.

It begins when you say: I am not that and that is not me. I'm only another that in the world. But I would like to know about that that. I find a use for that. It begins when you say: those are the terrors of women and children. Those are the poems of the sick. Philosophy always defeating itself with its own rules, chasing after chemistry with Wait, Wait! And holy men digging elephant traps. When you know this history, what do you know? You know the history of trying to know.

What then is Other—other-brother-mother . . .

❡33

When suffering is everywhere, that is of the nature of belief. When the leaders are corrupted, Pope or Commissar, nor do the people flicker an eyelash, that is of the nature of belief. When there are anniversaries of battle or martyrdom, that is of the nature of belief. When there is the slogan Credo quia absurdum or intellectual proof of the existence of God, that is of the nature of belief. When priests pray for victory and generals invoke heaven, when prisons fill with children, that is of the nature of belief. When the word *evil* appears in newspapers, *moral* in the mouths of policemen, *culture* in the prepared speeches of politicians, all that is of the nature of belief. Belief makes blood flow. Belief infects the dead with more belief. Now it flows in our veins. Now it floats in the clouds.

❡34

I am an atheist who says his prayers.

I am an anarchist, and a full professor at that. I take the loyalty oath.

I am a deviate. I fondle and contribute, backscuttle and brown, father of three.

I stand high in the community. My name is in *Who's Who*. People argue about my modesty.

I drink my share and yours and never have enough. I freeload officially and unofficially.

A physical coward, I take on all intellectuals, established poets, popes, rabbis, chiefs of staff.

I am a mystic. I will take an oath that I have seen the Virgin. Under the dry pandanus, to the scratching of kangaroo rats, I achieve psychic onanism. My tree of nerves electrocutes itself.

I uphold the image of America and force my luck. I write my own ticket to oblivion.

I am of the race wrecked by success. The audience brings me news of my death. I write out of boredom, despise solemnity. The wrong reason is good enough for me.

I am of the race of the prematurely desperate. In poverty of comfort I lay gunpowder plots. I lapse my insurance.

I am the Babbitt metal of the future. I never read more than half of a book. But that half I read forever.

I love the palimpsest, statues without heads, fertility dolls of the continent of Mu. I dream prehistory, the invention of dye. The palms of the dancers' hands are vermilion. Their heads oscillate like the cobra. High-caste woman smelling of earth and silk, you can dry my feet with your hair.

I take my place beside the Philistine and unfold my napkin. This afternoon I defend the Marines. I goggle at long cars.

Without compassion I attack the insane. Give them the horse-whip!

The homosexual lectures me brilliantly in the beer booth. I can feel my muscles soften. He smiles at my terror.

Pitchpots flicker in the lemon groves. I gaze down on the plains of Hollywood. My fine tan and my arrogance, my gray hair and my sneakers, O Israel!

Wherever I am I become. The power of entry is with me. In the doctor's office a patient, calm and humiliated. In the foreign movies a native, shabby enough. In the art gallery a person of authority (there's a secret way of approaching a picture. Others move off). The high official insults me to my face. I say nothing and accept the job. He offers me whiskey.

How beautifully I fake! I convince myself with men's room jokes and epigrams. I paint myself into a corner and escape on pulleys of the unknown. Whatever I think at the moment is true. Turn me around in my tracks; I will take your side.

For the rest, I improvise and am not spiteful and water the plants on the cocktail table.

* * *

When I dismissed you, friend, why did I do that? The Judas in me is strong. With an effort I regain my loyalty, and lose it again. These virtues incapacitate me. The solitude of the masochist is mine.

Albatross of a prize, you who married me to a newspaper, you who made me a government, why can't I thank you?

Kindness of deep hostility, my patience of a saint, endless capacity for love—mother, did I have the breast really? (But you gave me girls in your own likeness.)

This laissez-aller, this Traumdeutung—am I really a poet? Do I give a damn? That too I betray. I cross my fingers and exclude bedfellow death. I rub the icebox with my swimming thighs. I embrace the white rhinoceros; I propose to toilets.

What right have I to be healthy? What right have I to escape? And what is it I have escaped? I explore opportunities. (The rising sun sits on my other head. My cancer is blooming.)

I insist on the middle-aged poet. Brats of the drunken boat, centurions in the pay of Congress, gray and forgetful, purposefully stupid—God bless you, and Congress.

Marvelously recapitulating man, the child, reviving literature, invents religion. The dog flops on the floor with graceful disgust.

Goldfish, I loved you. When you died I cried. I'm no biologist. I did my best. I know. I overfed you. I was warned on the box. (The air-force officer has a tropical tank. His fishes glitter like a jewelry store.)

* * *

New York, my love, we never went to bed. (You never asked me.) New York, my Jewess, you read me Kierkegaard on the subway, standing up. I didn't give you a chance to kill me, N.Y.

Chicago, what did I do to you? What's another stab in the back, Chicago?

New York, killer of poets, do you remember the day you passed me through your lower intestine? The troop train paused under Grand Central. That line of women in mink coats handed us doughnuts through the smutty windows. They were all crying. For that I forgive New York. (We smuggled a postcard off at New Haven.)

Chicago, smothered in boredom and pigs: your Gothic universities, your Portuguese wines, your bad baseball.

New York, island of prisons. New York of a billion black Rimbauds. Chicago of dreamy cardinals.

What was it like, New York, when the skyscrapers were white? New York of Hart Crane. Harlem of Lorca.

Chicago of T.S. Eliot (his city). Chicago of bad impulses.

* * *

All things remain to be simplified. I find I must break free of the poetry trap.

The books I hunger for all always out, never to be returned: illuminations, personal bibles, diatribes, chapters denied acceptance in scripture, Tobit blinded by sparrows muting warm dung in his eyes, immense declarations of revolt, manuals of the practice of love.

I seek the entrance of the rabbit hole. Maybe it's the door that has no name.

My century, take savagery to your heart. Take wooden idols, walk them through the streets. Bow down to Science.

My century that boils history to a pulp for newspaper, my century of the million-dollar portrait, century of the decipherment of Linear B and the old scrolls, century of the dream of penultimate man (he wanders among the abandoned skyscrapers of Kansas; he has already forgotten language), century of the turning-point of time, the human wolf pack and the killing light.

* * *

Crazy-clean, our armies and bodies. Crazy-clean the institutions of the mind. Crazy-clean Washington, D.C.

The generals say: mop up, no sweat, cordon sanitaire, liquidate, flush, wipe out.

How many have escaped the prison of Art? Who has not been extradited? Through the blue grid of technique we read the wild faces.

Stanza means room, with bars on it. Form means shape, beaten and maimed. It is done, ingeniously done, immortally done. For a century or two it pleases and instructs.

Now and again, one of the slaves escapes. His eyes are put out with platinum hatpins.

To escape to America. How is it there? Do the bluecoats smile?

The little ones file into the classroom. The giggling dies down. They salute the flag. They bow their heads. Childhood is over. When the air raid sounds they crouch on the floor like Moslems. It's only for practice of course.

I tell the secret of the starving artist. A day after he died the chauffeurs knocked at the door.

Poets of early death, who overturned the boat? Physician John Keats, cure thyself!

Lists of the mad and bibles of the damned. Dictionaries of suicide, card indexes of the compulsive revolutionaries, Protestant cemeteries of sacred remains. Beautification of the Dutchman's ear. Under the dome of poetry an array of saints as broken as christological glass. Martyrology of prosodists. Mariolatry of Hebrews. Every twilight of the mind for sale.

Counterfeiters, defenders of hell-gate. The intentionally mad, aristocrats of the verb, apologists of exile, culture nationalists, founders of the Next Phase.

Studies of the decrease of light. Paintings of right angles. Poems with square edges. Literary quarterlies refined from steel.

*   *   *

The teacher recites her lesson: the poem lifts me; it tips my arrows. No matter the horror; it washes us, the blood-washed poem.

The teacher recites her lesson: this is reality; this is the ideal. This is the touch of God. My Muse, my mother, my fertile one. (A slow leak in the footnotes: the goddess bleeds apace.)

Why do you paint your lips? Is it time to eat?

The tigress rolls its cubs. The dainty sparrow, proletarian bird, lights on the horse turd, a golden bun. The mouse in the trap has exquisite fur. I touch it with my fingers before I lift it from the drawer on its well-made mouse-trap. The vertebra of the rattlesnake lies in the palm of my hand, a masterpiece of subtle bone. Where did you get it? The doll pouts: the child is learning a picture. You have to be taught to *read* a picture. The savage looks at the photograph of himself; he turns it sideways and upside-down. Why doesn't it register?

The class convenes in the library attic. I introduce myself and throw their books out of the window. We will write a poem together, I say. (I see the gothic in their eyes.) It turns out nicely.

My Utamaro is pea green. I see what Vincent saw.

Sunday cut into colored squares, *Chicago Tribune*, Japanese print of future generations, I collect your yellows and washy blues. Bold line of Dick Tracy, Lautrec of murder, sexless, decisive, one riddle solved, a fresh body produced. Your palindromes, a villain named Etah. Evil, said Carroll, is live spelled backwards.

Permanent orphan of generations, has daddy gone to fight the Communists with his private army and his diamond stickpin? Carrot-top orphan who still says *Hark!*

Cornbeef and cabbage man, pining for the brownstone days. Matronly Maggie with a rolling pin. (Pogo and Peanuts leave me cold.)

Sirens with black lips and identical faces. Fly-boys in the Orient; regulation uniforms.

Tillie and Mack in the Kinsey Collection. In New Guinea the Japanese propaganda drawings dropped from a Zero: Yank, this is what civilian is doing to your wife back home. (Showing what.) Colors of Utamaro.

Frank Merriwell at Yale. Tom the fun-loving Rover. Tom Swift and his electric grandmother (joke). Alger, Henty, S. S. Van Dine.

"Patterns" by Amy Lowell. And in Virginia, *Southern Prose and Poetry*.

Books for the sake of shelves. Encyclopedia of railroad engineering, sixty-seven volumes, fold-out plates of boilers, piston assembly. The Waverley novels, dark tomes maroon and brown to handle on a rainy day. Balzac complete, unread. *The Harvard Classics*, mean, unprovocative, *Veritas* stamped on the backbone.

* * *

Poem, is it de rigueur to descend to hell? Will you lose your pedigree?

How businesslike is convention. What slag the prodigies of the epic mind. How little human the heroes and angels.

Tell me again what tragedy is. I can never remember.

Because the king is a fool and the lady a bitch; because a woman butchers her children to spite her husband; or a man makes love to his mother by mistake—shall I descend to hell?

Because the dollar tips the scales; or certain languages are dead; the nobility bankrupt; because the government has awarded you teeth—shall I descend to hell?

I descend and find the usual evidence. And Paul made love to Frances and they burn forever.

Where are you taking me, Alighieri? I have a different religion. I go with Geoffrey to the house of April. Gottfried of Strassburg, give us the gutsy Tristan.

Children play on the gorgeous baldaquin, climbing the marble vines while the mothers kneel, eating the Body. The priest moves rapidly from mouth to mouth. Black and white, the barbaric tower rears over history. It's no playground.

The bloodshot Germans enter the Forum in shorts. Proudly they gaze on the fine destruction.

In Bombay the vegetarians storm the hotel: "You are eating the flesh of the god!" A dirty cow stands in the doorway of the office building. A Hindu gives it a kick in the rump and sends it off in the rain.

I teach the emotions. The head is a hugeness already. Sin is ruled out. A tropic laugh splits heaven up the middle.

The disciplinarians stalk between the flowers. The whips crash on the bitten fingernails. It's war from the start. The books are weighted with lead. The catechism demands more algebra. Down on your knees.

Who teaches manners of fear? Who teaches reverence of
wealth? Why so many books? What fabulous detail,
what attractive bindings! Did you take the Intelligence
Test this morning? Would you like to learn Russian?

The mind, the mind, cleaned like a car, purring like a fan.
And the feelings matted and stuck, scratching the lice
of love.

Do you hate your face? It is your sex you hate. Worship has
pigged your eyes.

*　　*　　*

O love, phenomenon of attention, hear me out! I hold the
shaving mirror to all:

To you at breakfast with folded newspaper,

You with the telephone in your hand and the glass name on
the door,

You the alumnus, recipient of telegraphed congratulations,

You on election night, you in the driver's seat,

You in dutiful coitus, you in social drunkenness, you in
parental storm;

At the cornerstone, near the triumphal arch, on the cruise
deck, in the ad for bitters,

In the photograph of the first lieutenant, signed "Ages ago,"

In the vestry room with the males and the white flower,

In the waiting room of the daffodil maternity ward,

At the elegant tent beside the open grave (the coffin glows
like a fine piano);

To you saluting, you baring your head, you holding the
scissor to the early rose—

Did you know the damasked walls gave way so rottenly, the gilted wood so mealy with fatigue?

Did you see the estates divided and plowed and the monstrous houses opened to view for your sad Sundays?

Aren't you the popular song of God in the formstone churches, you of ideals and virtues, responsible, lovable, disciplined, free?

Isn't it you you mutter against, with your fuzzed haircut in your wife's bosom?

Citizen, is your glorious revolution over and done with?

And you, my country, how does it feel to be They?

What are those objects on which our eyes are frozen?

Flag on the candy-factory grammar school;

Eternal light hung from a silver chain above the Ark in the synagogue;

Samurai sword in the French admiral's possession (to be given to a poet on a state occasion);

Rectilinear façade of Greek; font of the Hebrew; spittle of the christer contorting on the bare ground;

Finder of inscapes; critique of frameless abstractions; voyeurs of myth;

Hypnotized lovers; Napoleonic captains of copper mines; editors of quack compendia of knowledge;

All worshipers, all fanatics, all absorbed in the object which is really you,

You who descry the streamings of life as other and beyond;

You strapped to your muscles (is the culture-gag in your teeth?);

Altars, uniforms of every description, detritus of battles, delirium of ethics, codes of the good, new wars, new medals, new masterpieces forged for the market;

Heavy stone of your overturned lives, what crawling dreams!

What is it you are trying to become, men of my species?

Homo normalis, blind as a bat, that music you hear is coming from you. Where did you study the physics of the epic? What is this eternal conspiracy of distraction? Why are the sick the most articulate? Poetry weaving at the bar, go home. Somebody call a cab.

Who are these that compound the mystery? Tell me about the Dewey Decimal System.

Do something about the sour smell of schools. Call the Americans!

Herewith I abolish up and down. Future and past for those with radial vision.

Everything everywhere has been decided in everyone's favor.

I end on the dead level and peter out. Is it time for the curtain? Shall we applaud at the end of the second movement?

*　*　*

I love Nowhere where the factories die of malnutrition.

I love Nowhere where there are no roads, no rivers, no interesting Indians,

Where history is invented in the History Department and there are no centennials of anything,

Where every tree is planted by hand and has a private tutor,

Where the "parts" have to be ordered and the sky settles all questions,

Where travelers from California bitch at the backwardness
and New Yorkers step on the gas in a panic,

Where the grass in winter is gray not brown,

Where the population diminishes.

Here on the boundary of the hired West, equidistant from
every tourist office, and the air is washed by distance,
here at last there is nothing to recommend.

May no one ever attempt a recommendation; Chicago be as
far as Karachi.

Though the warriors come with rockets, may they fall off
the trucks.

May the voting be light and the clouds like a cruise and the
criminal boredom enter the district of hogs.

I love Nowhere where the human brag is a brag of neither
time nor place,

But an elephant house of Smithsonian bones and the white
cathedrals of grain,

The feeding-lots in the snow with the steers huddled in sym-
metrical misery, backs to the sleet,

To beef us up in the Beef State plains, something to look at.

                    *   *   *

To the poor (aux pauvres) crime alone (le crime seul) opens
(ouvre) les portes de la vie (the doors of life). Entire
libraries of music are hurled in the gutters: the G.I.'s
are looking for bottles. The Bavarian Venus is snatched
baldheaded.

I have a big sister; she has mighty breasts. She writes poems
for the immigration office. Her crotch is on the four-
teenth floor. La géante, la géante!

Standing at the pure white rail, stately we pass you, and the classes mingle as if by degree. At the last buoy the discreet signs begin to take effect: First Class, Second Class. My brazen sister swirling her nightgown, green as the spouts of Chartres. Her comb is combing my lice (but I have no lice). Her apron is hitched up in front. She stands on a full-sized bank.

Across the iambic pentameter of the Atlantic (the pilot dropped, the station wagon in the hold) we sail to the kingdom of Small. Is it cheaper there? Can I buy a slave?

This is the camera with the built-in lie. This is the lens that defies the truth. There's nothing for it but to write the large bad poem in middle-class magic. Poem condemned to wear black, be quoted in churches, versatile as Greek. Condemned to remain unsung by criminals.

II

Doctor Poet

⟨35

This Slavic typist had high cheekbones and gigantic mouth
and a voice like sleep. That Kyoto hostess naturally.
Marlene, Medea, and my wife, women proud as Tar-
tars, women with marvelous voices and big feet have
high cheekbones and dress their hair to a height.
In overcivilized rooms you will always find one or
two.

The Victorian houri had an oval face, a drooping silkiness
of flesh like ottomans. She melted away in the dawn
of the century. A drunken poet roars out across the
room: are you a tit man or an ass man? I mumble in
reply: high cheekbones.

Verlaine compares the buttocks and the breasts: buttocks the
holy throne of the indecencies. Breasts savored by
drunken lips and the tongue. Buttocks with their ravine
of rose and somber shadow, where desire prowls
when it goes crazy. Breasts proud and victorious,
breasts heavy and powerful. Buttocks, beloved cush-
ions, with a voluptuous fold for your face or your sex.
O holy quaternity of sacred breasts and august buttocks.

Poets with high cheekbones, Rimbaud, Pasternak.

¶36

In the second-best hotel in Tokyo the chambermaids are
chasing the chamberboys. Laughter tinkles up and
down the halls. The elevator girls sing it when they
say: ten floor, please; seven floor, please (their faces
like gardenias). The cashier's fingers race back and
forth over the counting frame.

In the first-best Western-style hotel in Kyoto I describe to
the barmaid how to make a Bloody Mary, and am
proud. I walk through the fish market with the editor
of *The Kenyon Review*. The fishes are displayed like
masterpieces. This is more beautiful than the Louvre.

I fall in love with the torii gate, graceful salmon arms, the
light rust color. From now on it's my Parthenon.
The wooden golden palace floats on its pond. The
nightingale floors warn me of my assassins. I sleep like
an Oriental.

Zen is on the verge of being discovered. We climb to the famous abstract garden and study the sand designs and the rocks. To my companion I say: how do they fix it without messing it up? He laughs at my westernization.

As for the haiku, you can make it tough. It isn't exactly a valentine, except in the States.

❪37

I wait up for the movies of my war, late, late at night on television. It comes with crackling fanfare, with faulty memory for the facts of life. But it's true enough to keep me awake, staring in the dark, groping my way back to my war. It's true, not true to life. I study the hair of the sweethearts that hangs to their shoulders (yours was like that), the square-shouldered dresses, junk jewelry and all. Farewells, convoys, dawn bombardments, palm trees nestling Japs in their crotches. I hear the faded propaganda message on the dying lips of the handsome actor; my heart pounds to the pull of the flag in the artificial wind. And the next assault, and the next. And the homecoming. Homecoming destroys me: I weep. (I'm glad you are asleep.)

Those movies under the moon in New Guinea, helmets clanking quietly in the mud as we watched the giantess dancing our heartbreak. Movies shut off while the air raid passed, rot of coconuts, our own bad sweat asserting itself till the dream returned. Movies of the moving thigh and the honey-thick ballad heavy as ether. Mis-

taken-identity movies, pie-throwing movies, no movies
of war in the war zone. These are saved for my middle-
aged bed.

¶38

The poet takes the voyage to the New Cytherea. Fifty miles
from little Papeete he and his girl have rented a
thatched hut. He says the name of the district over
and over: Taravao, Taravao. The hut is right on the
beach; water laps at the pilings. The whole front opens
crazily out and is propped up by a stake. The roof is
pandanus, very brown and dusty, a house of straw.
No sooner have they entered when the poet grabs up
a witch's broom and begins to sweep. The girl hangs
batiks on the wall. There are spiders big as your hand.
Frozen with terror the poet smashes them.

Over the water rises Moorea, blue-mauve with lots of red,
as the painter saw it. The poet sweeps and arranges
like a woman. He lays out books. The hut is ready
at last; they lean out of the open wall and worship the
world. They make love on the crunchy bed. Later the
natives bring bananas as a gift. Their movements are
slow and peaceful, their French is soft and broad. Inside the coral reef the swimming is perfect. They shop
in Papeete. They bank at the Bank of Indo-China.
Everything is exotic, even the nuns. At the Post Office
a crowd of French sailors are arguing grimly. Spain
is at war with itself. It has started today. It is even
here.

There is only one movie: *Tabu* by Murnau. The natives return to it like a church. We go there. It is great like literature.

¶39

Wood for the fireplace, wood for the floor, what is the life span? Sometimes before I lay the log on the fire I think: it's sculpture wood, it's walnut. Maybe someone would find a figure in it, as children find faces in the open fire (I never have). Then I lay it on the flames like a heretic, where it pauses a moment, then joins in the singing. There's oak in this cord too. My floor is oak. I watched them lay this floor, for a vastly slower fire. The grooved pieces are fitted together; it's more like a game than work; there are many choices. The grain falls arbitrarily, dark streaks and light, dots and dashes, swirls and striped shields.

Dead wood can last forever (is it dead?). Dead wood glows in palaces, rosy and dark as masterpieces. I worship wood, split my own logs in the driveway, using a maul and iron wedges. The cracking-apart is hard and sweet. I touch wood for my superstition, using five fingers as an extra precaution. My gods would all be wood if I had gods, not stone or gold or Peter's smooth-kissed toe.

In woodless Italy houses are built without a sound, no ring of hammer on nail or wood. All is quiet, stone laid upon stone, rubble, cement, tufa, travertine, tile. Rarely

you see some show-off house of wood, exotic among
the blinding stucco, soft among the cool and stony
facings, the marbly infinitude.

¶40

In a single motion, a snap of the hand, you take the white
bishop with your black knight, taking-replacing. It's
neat, like trigger work, the click of the chessmen
speaking in passing, like the hammers of empty re-
volvers. Well, uncle who taught me the courtly game,
who sat with experts over silent boards, I never made
the grade. I play as badly now that I'm gray as I did
those years before I shaved. My chess plateau was
never a high one. No matter. Still, I can beat my
children when we play, which is practically never.
When we do, and I capture a pawn or a rook with
a click, taking-replacing, I think of your house, the
pipes, the dice, the trinkets, curios ("novelties" they
were called). Your business, pipes and novelties, not
very lucrative but treasure-trove of kids. Your sad
blond face, so kind, politically angry, yet easy to
laugh—you were not at home in this country, scholar
manqué, drifting apart from the richer and richer
relations. Your foreign accent perhaps, your synagogue training leading to nowhere. There was that
about you of the disengaged, the saint (using the word
advisedly and well), the Jewish radiance of a Chagall.
The rich ones never played chess, the poetry of war,
nor grunted sadly at the news. In America, scholars
are thrown into the street or made to stand behind

cool counters, thumping, unthumping the mighty bolts
of cloth. Good cloth at that but not for the torah.

❦ 41

Not at all my favorite author, Kipling described Chicago
once: the water is the water of the Hooghly, and the
air is dirt. And as famous a poet of New England
whom I drive to the station: it's a grand city. (*Grand*,
a nineteenth-century word.)

Under its permanent umbrella of travail, Chicago swirls in
grit. Smuts drift in the sky, penetrate window glass,
light on petals of window-box flowers, turning gera-
niums pansy-black. All is charred, all is furred with
dirt, the sky winter and summer streaked like the sky-
light of the grandest railroad station, basilicas of
practical kings.

But now we take leave forever by car, driving in early
morning south, miraculously out from under the soiled
umbrella, south and more south in the dead blue winter
light, south and west in the snow-light, till the snow
rots in Arkansas, then west again, the holy direction.

Far from the Chicago cave, spring comes facing toward summer, such summer as happens only in one place in a
given country.

There is a rise (where is it on the map?), on one side America
and on the other, California. There you look down on
promised advertisements of green come true, green for
the eating, money-green, and the rows of the royal

palm for welcome, official, frightening. The Californians live in California. The money groves are green. America is a suburb of California et cetera et cetera.

America is Hooghly.

❡42

Little tendon, tiny as a hair—tinier, the surgeon said—they couldn't catch you on the operating table. Three hours we lay there, wrist neatly slit open—I can't even find the scar—while they caught you and lost you, caught you and lost you, and then, more or less sure, caught you again (but didn't).

And now one finger doesn't work so well. I can't make a fist with my left hand, and it's hard to pick up change. (I'm left-handed, of course.) It would have to be my favorite hand that I pushed through the door glass (one drink too many).

But how I slept, truth serum in my veins, happily missing the glitter and click of hemostats. And woke to your hard professional slaps in the face, in Recovery, nurse. You must have been late for your date, good-looking nurse; your make-up was perfect when I saw you at last, and you had stopped bawling my name in my ear, like a character in *Alice in Wonderland*, stopped letting me have the flat of your hand.

Arm in sling, hand in aluminum brace, I lecture and teach while the tendon sleeps. It's not worth fixing really.

I'm not a pianist or, as you put it, doctor, a Swiss watchmaker. But a dancer one night says to me at a party: Are you disfigured? (Only a dancer would use a word like that.)

❪43

Proud of my half-education now, that drove me bookish in my youth from daily shame, I proudly say I know, I actually know, what education is. And now that I know, I know I shall not have one, nor am I sure I want one, considering the cost and the late date. In any case, we never have the chance but once—twice at the most.

Education is a family tree on which to hang your gods. Gods of names or dates, gods of battles or famous humanitarian mistakes; or gods themselves; or (in Chicago) Great Ideas. But the tree's the thing. Without a tree, even a green sapling, where will you hang your myths, your dying Gauls, your Christmas stocking?

Higher education is a higher tree; it spreads its branches over time and clime, or shoots sky-high in forests impervious to termites. And on this staggering frame the gods hang down in grape clusters of grace, dripping design like Hindu temples, leaking and writhing for the glacial pinnacles of Dark Age cathedrals, speeding in fabulous monotony up verticals of Manhattan glass.

Growth of the dead on the trellis of life; classification of friend and foe; heraldry, orthography, communications: education is when you know where to hang something.

Universitas Nebraskensis it says on the copybook. And on
The Harvard Classics—Veritas!

⟨44

Third Class, *Queen Mary*, late December on the high Atlantic.
The storm is fabulous. Seas run to the height of the
promenade deck where picture windows are smashed.
The ocean frowns like elephant hide and has a texture
almost smooth. In the dining room I am sat with Miss
Cohen at a table for two. (The English keep races together.) I tell her proudly that this was my troopship.
Proudly I describe the Mary in wartime: gray from
stem to stern, all ports and windows blacked, the mon-
ster zigzagging from Boston to the Sydney Heads.
Forty days and forty nights, Key West, Rio, Cape-
town, south almost to Little America, north to New
South Wales. Now it seems quiet and empty, clean and
well-kept as a cemetery, even in this great storm. —Ah,
this is different, says Miss Cohen: we are paying for
this.

We are paying for this!

The server is polite and clean. He tends us in the mighty
empty ship. The tablecloth is white, the silver silver.
The waiters call me Sir. This voyage I am Sir. I pay.

In the vulgarity of poetic justice, Miss Cohen is knocked from
her chair by a skyscraper sea. I visit her in the hospital.
She is ugly; I like her. I say to myself, she offended the
god of the storm.

❡45

Autumn reminds me that you bit my lips, excellent nurse of
the most famous hospital, with puffy eyes and adver-
tisable rear. North of beautiful Baltimore, in valley
taverns, reminiscent of imagined England, we watched
from the rail fence the blessing of hounds. At the place
of our date you made a pass at my just-married friend
in the face of his bride. She is dark and full, a Renoir
woman with Brooklyn accent. You are light and thin,
lacking in humor or observation. How slowly the dark
one moves while you engage her husband in jokes and
hugs and public thigh-pushes, all thoroughly insincere.
Till the bride's laughter congeals in her throat and
suddenly she is flying hands and knives of fingernails
slashing wickedly at your soft attractive face, your
sleepless eyes with albino lashes.

At night in the improvised bed by the living-room fire in the
stone cottage you bite and use your nails. Afterwards
you want me to stay inside you the entire night, even
asleep. I laugh, I beg. Instead of whispering *darling*
you whisper (with such conviction) —*you worm!*

❡46

Priests and Freudians will understand. In the throttling
Papuan heat, even the rain is hot, even the rain carries
the rot smell. Lying in mud or in soaked hammocks the
soldiers stew and joke and empty their dead minds.
Deprived of love and letters and the sight of woman,
the dead mind rots.

Who sent this missal soft and black, with iridescent gold and five silk ribbons sewn in the binding: red, silver, blue, green, purple? Two thousand pages mica-thin, like two millennia of daily shame.

Nearby, the natives make themselves strong by drinking sweat of warriors, eating fingernails coated with human blood. Priests and Freudians comprehend. And now I learn the missal prayers. I set up mental prayer wheels and spin them with the whips of fear. Help me, Freudians and priests: when I say the proud Hail Mary, the serpent takes me in the groin.

I seek the chaplain in his tent. Father, convert me. He looks at me and says: You must excuse me, sergeant. I have a furlough coming up.

When I say the Hail Mary I get an erection. Doesn't that prove the existence of God?

⁊47

Next to my office where I edit poems ("Can poems be edited?") there is the Chicago Models Club. All day the girls stroll past my door where I am editing poems, behind my head a signed photograph of Rupert Brooke, handsomer than any movie star. I edit, keeping one eye peeled for the models, straining my ears to hear what they say. In there they photograph the girls on the bamboo furniture, glossies for the pulsing façades of night spots. One day the manager brings me flowers, a huge and damaged bouquet: hurt gladiolas, overly open roses, long-leaping ferns (least hurt), and bruised carnations. I accept the gift, remainder of last night's opening (where?), debut of lower-class blondes. I distribute the flowers in the other poetry rooms, too formal-looking for our disarray.

Now after every model's bow to the footlights the manager brings more flowers, hurt gladiolas, overly open roses, long-leaping ferns and bruised carnations. I edit poems to the click of sharp high heels, flanked by the swords of lavender debut, whiffing the cinnamon of crepe-paper-pink carnations of the bruised and lower-class blondes.

Behind me rears my wall of books, most formidable of human barriers. No flower depresses me like the iris but these I have a fondness for. They bring stale memories over the threshold of the street. They bring the night of cloth palm trees and soft plastic leopard chairs, night of sticky drinks, the shining rhinestone hour in the dark-blue mirror, the peroxide chat of models and photogenic morn.

Today the manager brinks all gladioli. A few rose petals lie in the corridor. The mail is heavy this morning.

¶48

The Personnel Manager blandly said: They complain of your staring—and named names. The one backed like a horse, very high in the rump; the flat-chested one with exquisite calves; the small one, "blue-eyed and blond," with curves in every direction and deep chiaroscuro make-up.

Everyone tells me I have beautiful eyes, or is it brows. (What are brows?) Women admire my thick lashes. I fear you, Personnel Manager, though my daddy is your superior. I feel inferior to you in these questions. Yet if you knew the word *voyeur* you would understand that I too am a Personnel Manager. I too am bald. I too am objective. I too entice with the guttural.

Nevertheless I will lower my eyes and play the game. I will learn a little of the love life of offices, not much but enough. You want me to see without being seen. This lesson burns me deeply. He seems to say with staggering banality: The criminal is one who is caught.

❨49

You sat me down and taught me how to edit. I was shy with the thick blue pencil in my hand. Begin the assault, you grinned. But I was afraid to violate those hard-earned words. Someone had promised them freedom of the page. You show me your results: fine diagonal slashes, headline Z's, the graceful swirls of transposition, question marks hooked into weedy thought. So this is what you do: you make them say exactly what you think they mean. You drive out of the bushes of language their naked shame of thought. Under the cold fluorescent lamp you exact the evidence of words. What's left is strong and little.

This is a paragraph. A paragraph is a sonnet in prose. A paragraph begins where it ends. A paragraph may contain a single word or cruise for pages. Good writing rids itself of style, sanctifies no grammar, is silent more than it speaks. Most writing is bad because the writer never sits down to think until he sits down to write. Most writing is dishonest because the writer doesn't believe what he writes but is honestly trying to find out. Most writing is at the expense of the reader, a kindly fellow who would like to believe you.

Here is a spy report from a German woman living in New York and spying on Nazis. We don't know which side she is on. Figure it out.

❡50

August Saturday night on the Negro street the trolleys clang and break sweet dusty smoke. Cars hoot meaningless signals. The air is in a sweat of Jim Crow gaiety, shopping, milling, rubbing of flesh, five miles of laughter in white Baltimore. The second floor dance hall has a famous trumpet. You can't move on the floor, which rolls like waves and is in actual danger of giving way. The temperature adds to the frenzy. There is no pause in the jump and scream of the jazz, heat waves of laughter, untranslatable slang. The dancing is demotic, terpsichorean. It's like a war of pleasure. It's the joy of work. The fatigue is its own reward.

Across the street in the corner drug store where whiskey is sold and every blandishment of skin, a teeming Negress crowds at the perfume counter, big arms like haunches and bosom practically bare. She laughs with her friends above the cut-glass bottles with Frenchified names and recently invented colors. She purchases a sizeable vial of some green scent, pays green dry money, unstoppers the bottle and dumps the entire load between her breasts! O glorious act of laughter in the half-serious bazaar of the Jew-store!

ℂ51

I perform in the drug-store window, stretching into neatly
folded draperies the rubbery and lavender crepe paper.
Two little children watch as I empty a box of tacks into
my mouth and tread softly between two huge glass
vessels, one filled with blue water, one filled with red.
The tack hammer is magnetized. I put it to my lips and
catch a tack, point outward, swiftly fastening the flimsy
drapes this way and that. Rosettes I make, flounces,
valance at the top, then set the beautiful cardboard
actress up, life-size face selling perfume or soap. My
eyes dizzily graze her eyes.

In hardware windows comic displays of insecticides. In a
thousand neighborhood bars I fashion crinkly curtains
of red to frame vast mirrors. Always a jocular free
beer, warming off-color jokes with the woman. Bars
for workingmen. I am almost a workingman I tell myself.

I am a worker I tell myself. Ils sont dans le vrai (for I am
literary). My uneasiness with salesmen, terror of the
rich. I have seven vocabularies: they change with the
locale. The city itself changes: here it is London, here
it is Paris; here it is eighteenth-century. I haunt the
second-hand bookshops or visit a one-dollar woman. It's
a tossup.

ℂ52

One by one my troops desert. A hair at a time. One by one and
there is no return. Yesterday it was dark and soft, un-

noticeable as a pore. Today it sticks up at a crazy angle,
bristling with what act of rebellion. Yesterday a
tendril, a decoration, a vestige of biology, today barbed
wire. I count them all till I've lost count. I count from
the top of my head. The revolution started in that
sector.

In the sole world of the self that is how it happens. One cell
revolts against the general harmony. The body's
bourgeois security is threatened. The government gives
a perceptible shudder. One cell alone goes off, giving
the finger sign of obscenity. Urchins and panhandlers
cheer him on. In a moment he is making speeches.
Then the police, then the militia, soon the victorious
grave.

Rising crooked on my arm, darting wickedly out of my eye-
brows, blanching my chest like sun, what do you want,
blackmailers, professional mourners. I see you starting
down my arms like lice, infiltrating to the very wrist.
How far will you go? When will order be restored.
Halfway measures for fops and actors, black dye,
tweezers, cuticle scissors. Shall I give you away? I
know your little game. I saw it in the bath the other
day. This plot would tickle Rabelais. A pubic hair
turned silver gray!

¶53

The Bach *Partitas* saved my life. Floating in fever over
Cincinnati, I felt the soft piano hammers sounding my
chest, my soul, my balls. Ancient and skillful fingers
worked their way—genius of chiropractic, I am un-

cracked again! Crucified on silk rope ladders that tickle the back of my neck I sail down blazing sea lanes with old poems that disgust me nowadays. I'm not sick enough for a reconciliation. Maybe I'm only malingering. The doctor says through a brandy snifter as big as my head: the virus yes, but somebody is bothering you. He's telling my fortune.

Waves of activity spring from the phonograph: the left-hand figure is deep in my bowels. Yes, there's a student wrecking my work. I'm too much of a coward to kick him out. There's a girl who was burned in a fire; I fear for her sanity. Or a Quaker lady bound for jail; and a jazz musician. I've lost the clue for keeping them together.

They used to call it brain fever or broken heart. Medicine was metaphorical in those days. But one can train a deadly disease to run your affairs while you're away. You adopt it while it is young, shower it with affection, give it the confidence of education.

Stay in bed for a week. Learn the *Partitas*. This music forgives me. Love of simplicity, fear of the obvious, at bottom the dread of being an impostor. Is it ever too late to denounce? The music is playing me—the wrong approach as usual.

₵54

Mr. Cochran flags the train. One man with a flag can stop all that steam and steel and make it roll again. He sits in a doll house by the railroad track and we go there to keep him company. All day he whittles and tells us stories.

He whittles us fine sticks with designs. His favorite
pattern is pitting with an awl. A stick of wood becomes
a talisman with stars, indentations, smooth and mag-
ical. When we go home for our nap we show our
treasures.

Two Boy Scouts climb the switch tower to pay a visit to Mr.
Carter. He sits at rows of lights and black-handled
levers, dangerous to touch. Everything up here is
dangerous and thrilling. Mr. Carter whittles people,
naked people with private parts. Sometimes there are
two people stuck together in crazy positions. It's quite
a museum up here. When the lift-gates clang and drop
and the traffic piles up, we all look down on the open
automobiles, girls in bathing suits going to the beach.
The tower trembles with the thunder of the freight
train.

This figurine of steatite speaks to me. Narrow eyes, thick
lips, flat nose, deep carven beard and hair, deep clover-
pattern of vestment. Chalcolithic of Mohenjo-Daro.

In the junk shop I ask to buy the life-size wooden horse. It
came from a saddler's of the sod-house days. But it's
not for sale except to a museum. We go away, my
daughter and I, with a milking stool, nice near the
fireplace.

℄55

Every day when I walk by the immense publishing company,
I know they are rolling out enormous medical tomes.
And I know, like a secret, they are printing my book of
poems. In front of the rounded plate-glass windows I

am Raskolnikov. Yet I don't affront the editor: it's purely a business transaction to him.

I want the title page just so. I show a D. H. Lawrence title page, boldface British, unmistakable. The rest in book type, untechnological. The conventional length of sixty-four pages, poetry-size. The binding maroon.

In gold I also use my middle initial but spelled out JAY. J is for Jacob. My father dropped his first name Israel. My son is named Jacob. Upper-class Jews call him Jack. My father-in-law's name was Jack, probably Jacob.

The act of a book to hold in the hand is its own reason. The little defiance of a book of poems. Bludgeoning and recompense of uncles.

¶56

In with four others, like a Third-Class stateroom. I am the first in uniform, worse luck. I name my poems with the round word Noun. In the introduction I say: my house, my street, my city. I lash out against the word America, word of the soft white bread of song, word of poets with two telephones. I volunteer to overthrow the government of critics.

One of my verse-mates will carry the young on their backs up above skyscrapers. He points below to the city of love. Him I salute. One will translate the freezing *Herodiade*. One will disappear from the lists. One will engage in a theory of the verb.

This noun, my burning-glass of detail, recklessly sentimental. I elegize the death of an anarchist woman and praise the bosomy fatness of a car. Again and again I attack Virginia. They have sent me here; "they will pay for it handsomely." All the same, I have nothing better to do. In a matter of days the guarded train to the battle-gray ship. Helmeted soldiers stand at the switches in the Boston yards, rifles between their legs. The books are heavy in my duffle bag.

¶57

The best book has a bad finality. The best book closes too many rooms. The best poem clicks like a box: you have made yourself a neat little trap, a hideaway with wall-to-wall rhyme. Praises of passers-by, equivalent of riches. Double feeling of triumph and depression, like one who has reached the mountain top. He notes with surprise that he is going down. Better not think about it.

The book becomes a personal establishment, a house with a plaque. Here at last is a base of operations. Better not think about it. He goes to the triumph of cocktails.

Name in the papers, what does that mean? Flattering misunderstandings of journalists, pegs for book reviewers, once in a novel, mentioned like a landmark. The business suit of his mind is pressed. I will scuff my shoes.

Contact with famous names. Private dreams of murdering the king of the wood. Rumors of honors and insults. Settling of pride like calcium deposits. Hardening of the jaw and sweetness of the eye.

Thrice printed in England, the holy land.

¶58

There's the green fire of the tropics and the white fire of steel
screaming and the purple fire of the blood religion.
Under this tricolor the poet writes, of all places in
Malinowski's island. Girls of eight, Kagwalosa, Baka-
kubla, maybe they are nympholepts. A soldier is shot:
did he shoot himself? it's time for an elegy anyway.
The women march to the water-well in the morning,
barebreasted. We make a study of the human melons.
They wash their yaws in their own drinking water.
Poems about Christmas, poems about Jews: what is it
he is trying to betray under the palm trees scratchy
with rats? He writes his only love poem. The exotic
danger and the length of time, the old chestnuts Pity
and Terror, Form and Content, Good and Evil, Love
and Hate: simple chords vibrate all the way to Manhattan where dreams come true. Rumors of other poets
of war, many at every landing stage, many in every
theater of war. The farthest from home is the luckiest.
Thanks to Jesus, thanks to the Rabbi, thanks to the
buggy thatch and the loud hibiscus, the book sails to
the heart of the prize. There's a ticker-tape welcome
of experts somewhere. The Navy buys an entire edi-
tion! History, propitiated, smiles with golden teeth. It's
only a matter of time. He flatly refuses to be killed in
battle.

¶59

Collecting oneself is like moving to another country. Take
this, store that. This poem may come in handy in
Kansas. There's one for curious rabbis and young girls.

To scramble the chronology make an A B C arrangement. Start with Adam and Eve (to read last at recitals). Is it as much as you thought? There is never enough and never little enough.

Photograph album lying on the grass, the wind reads you lazily. The wind thumbs my episodes. A few drops of rain splatter my years. There's plenty of sighing for impossibles. I love the wine stains on certain accidental poems, pale purple Matisse wallpaper. Who spilled that? Some faces are already repressed. Here is a fallen hand, poked by a stick. The usual insectivora worry my pocket watch. Plenty of castration symbols (you know what *that* means). Dirty-dog poems baying at the moon-mother. Dedicated to three nicknames.

¶60

The molasses of lecturing is sweet and the rum of polemic is good for the stomach. I write prose to find out what I think. Then it is printed. The whole business is irresponsible. But it's getting somewhere: if the polished paragraph won't work I'll pick up mud. There are no rules in this game. You can skewer a king or throw him in the pig pond.

They pay me handsomely to think mephitically. It's myth I'm after, and historicity. Picasso gets it in the neck. He's classical, he's cold, his mind is a factory. He's rich and Red and shrewd as nails. There's your bourgeois artist to a T. You want a Picasso? Kiss a woman with your eyes open. You want a nose on the back of your neck? Authentic cold cuts, eyes of interior decorator. Plenty of myth, plenty of history, with a side order of Spanish blood in the sand. Plates!

¶61

Always the character who yells, I insist, I insist on being a
Jew! (Can't you forget it? Isn't it obsolete? Isn't it
faking the evidence?) I insist, I insist. Everyone is
offended by a different nuance of the word. Rimbaud
called it his nigger book. I'm kinky and horny and
greasy too. Spit in my face and hang me up to dry.

¶62

I said to Ignotus in the shadow of the peristyle: I will carry
your message *to take the side of the child forever*. And
I stood on the banks of the Ohio River and I used cun-
ning and loud-mouth. There I rocked the solid Dagons
on the block-letter pedestals and they crashed down on
the city (I think). And I sat by the golf course and
drank Scotch and in one afternoon evoked a new god.
And graybeards milled at the corners with sullenness.
Doors of reformatories flew open. Red lights were hung
at the porches of churches. And I wept for clowns. And
a female secretary at a publisher's office asked to be
arrested. And a famous scholar lunged at my face with
a desk spindle. And thus we proclaimed Christmas
on earth, Ignotus.

These things take time, or an earthquake. People are reluctant
to relinquish their holdings in libraries. The children
themselves are unreliable: why shouldn't they be sus-
picious. Their hiding places are known by the international police. Their telephone wires are cut at the
drop of a hat. In every closet the hooded sisters and

the reversible fathers. It's that or the doctor boiling his
knives. There's one good thing about the culture gods:
they're fresh out of poison (I think). Unless they're
planning our final Fourth of July. They have a place to
go. They always do.

❡63

Your book about my books, which I'm the only reader of. O
book that's absolutely mine, that I didn't have a hand
in. Mirror of my Narcissus years, music box, what if I
stop now? List of notices that brought me nights of
delirium, ecstasy, fury, heartbreak, mirror broken and
magically joined together without a flaw. History of
me which only I can read. And you, my author, what
thanks or regrets shall I give? You took me alive, hands
tied behind, delivered me to the marshal of degrees.
There on the platform where all things fall through, I
went down in operatic flames. In velvet cape and
sword of pen, I accepted.

Incapacity for sincerity reminds me of an oral question:
Molière, était-il sincère? (What in the name of God is
prose?)

Phone book of myself, I will call you up.

❡64

The creativeness of the artist is a most efficient technique
for liquidating guilt and re-establishing the function of

*pity . . . This mental organization is a fortunate one
for the artist in the man; but it is an unfortunate one for
the man in the artist since it afflicts him with his emotional
immaturity, exquisitely narcissistic character, maladjust-
ment to life, and recurrent neurotic depressions . . .
Harry B. Lee, M.D.*

When the last door closes in the wintry afternoon at the main
gate of the asylum, you enter your car with a sigh.
Behind you lies the only world you know. Those in the
traffic are on the waiting list. I'll tell you all I know. I
owe it to someone I've forgotten.

I

The father says: Don't play with that boy any more. He looks
unhealthy. He masturbates. The father says: Look at
his eyes. Read this medical book, says the father. The
medical book reads like a Bible: You will surely be
driven to insanity and early death. Your muscles will
flab, eyesight fail, softening of the spine. Don't touch
it, whatever you do. Terror and hurt. I look at my
friend and see only my friend. I study my own face.
In summer when they paint my room the bed is moved
from the wall and the wall is spattered with dirty
dreams. —My friend! My friend!

II

When he grows up he will be a doctor himself. Then he will
be an analyst. But this afternoon in the attic after
school we take our pants down. There is a sickening
jar of his mother's cold cream and the foreign feel of
each other. A generation later at dinner he reminds me
of our curiosity, laughing enjoyably.

III

On certain nights the parents' door is locked and I try not to
think about it. In my father's top drawer I have seen
the delicate powdered skins and the filthy pamphlet
with real photographs.

IV

My son, only eight days old, what insanity has led me to hand
you over to them for the sacrifice! The blood spurts;
they are praying in Hebrew. The foreskin is bought
back. Coward that I am, I insist on making you a Jew.
Someone says: Besides, it's hygienic.

V

I'll make you pity me. I'll make you cry. (I do that to all the
girls.) I write a letter of fourteen pages; I do that every
day. I talk on the phone till midnight, I forget about
what. Flooded with tears we make a kind of love.
That's as far as I'll go. (You'd think I was the girl.)

VI

I was just married, you were just divorced, mother. I am back
from the Army. I take you in my arms. I think I forget
who everyone is. Because of the tears and confusion I
put my hand on your breast. I swear it was an accident.
I doubt if you noticed. I was the last to marry. Probably you didn't want me to. Trouble ahead.

VII

I refuse to cut my father off. (Incapable of bad feeling.) Once
I dream about his second wife, labia majora like a
horse's saddle. At the Christmas party in the falling-
apart office, daddy kisses the secretary, which is okay
except that I'm in love with her. She is engaged to a
lawyer. I send her a poem of intense self-pity.

VIII

The rabbi has contempt for me. He gives me the blessing
(that's part of his job) but the audience is small.
Grandpa has died. My watch isn't as thin as my
brother's. Mediocrity is my middle name. Then I fail
algebra and fall in love with the tutor, whose name is
Miss Hamlet. They expect nothing of me but jokes.
One brilliant son is enough.

IX

Teasing my sister is abetted by my teaching her to smoke.
Her girl friend has hard little breasts which I play with
when she will let me (she pretends not to notice). Out
of how many I've known only one girl with nipples in
actual erection. Whose fault? Disgust. I was bottle-fed
I think.

X

Four boys come out of the pine clearing. We build a fire to
roast the potatoes. Together we defecate on the railroad tracks. Extreme satisfaction.

XI

Only five, I steal a small packet of candy from the grocery
store. They are called Charms. I am caught; I was not
sure it was wrong. It is mother who makes me cry,
yet she is love-worthy.

XII

I change the bad marks on my report card. Later I have to
change them back. The punishment is severe: a lecture
by Uncle Paul, followed by the belt from daddy. Monstrous shame followed by forgiveness. He comes to my
room at night to soothe me. Scenes of reconciliation
break me to pieces.

XIII

The handsome flyer is off to the R.A.F. He knows I cuckold
him. He is shot down in his first operation. I try to
feel guilty but can't.

XIV

Without warning I fire a woman from her life's work. She
turns away without a sound; her lips are bloodless.
I know she will blame my wife instead of me.

XV

Purely out of boredom I involve others in a "question of
principle." I defame the University in passing. Then
I allow myself to be persuaded to withdraw the ac-
cusations (which are valid). I apologize to the con-
spirators, not to the injured.

XVI

Terrified by my table manners I refuse to eat after having
accepted the invitation. (As guest of honor I never
know when to get up.) Someone thinks I have religious
scruples about food.

XVII

That soldier in the shower has a beautiful uncircumcised
penis. I recall it for years. The fairy being sent home
from New Guinea (Section VIII) is drunk and abusive
to me at my desk. I am writing a poem. He accuses me
of not being queer. I am almost hurt.

XVIII

At the publishers' convention I sneer at the liberalism of
librarians. They would like to see everything printed,
obscene or not. That day I stand for morals.

XIX

Having canceled the rest of my tour for the State Department
I find I owe them several hundred dollars for travel
advances. I delay the payments indefinitely and take
several years to repay them. Meanwhile I take pleasure
telling about it at parties.

XX

I insist on a Christmas tree for the children and am infuriated
by it. I try to make it a work of art. The children sit
and hug their knees after it is consummated. I allow
myself all the wrong connotations.

XXI

My hostess drinks too much and asks me to hide a full glass
of bourbon behind the bookcase. I delight in helping.
Daughter of a famous man. No malice in this.

XXII

Ashamed of the valve-slap of my vulgar Ford on the Italian
beach (afraid I am letting my country down!) I keep
the radio running at all times. When the muscular
dystrophy child dislocates her thumb, I speed her to
the hospital at a hundred miles an hour. When it is
over I kiss her. I'm called simpatico, and like it. I
weep.

XXIII

I lose at poker on purpose and it takes all my salary. I have
read Freud on Dostoyevsky: I scatter my seed—Why
don't I want to win? I have never won at a game, any
game. Let somebody else take the responsibility.

XXIV

The moment a person becomes my Boss I am abject. Com-
munication is definitely impaired. Fear-love never in-

terested me. It's one or the other. Bosses are fear gods. Love gods I love, the older the better.

XXV

Iconography of physique, very individual, impossible to construct in conversation, virtually impossible to find. But the main ingredient: a certain expression of the eyes and mouth. A busted nose will help. Breadth of the tongue.

XXVI

Out of *The Hundred and Twenty Days of Sodom* two images. The most beautiful ass in France (unfortunately not described) and the superior sweat of the redhead's arm-pits. Benign tertiary convulsion: shouting and bellowing of orgasm like a bullfight.

XXVII

The misprints in my early books have never been corrected. "Zen."

XXVIII

My reputation for sincerity is sincere. I am sincere. You are sincere. My capacity for belief is convincing. I could be an Arab or an Ultra, a Communist or a Republican. Honestly.

XXIX

Longing for the Primitive I survive as a Modern, barely.

XXX

The ultimate absurdity: no fear of nonrecognition. No instinct for survival. No regrets for the future. No plans for the present. Read positively: I am what I am. My chances here and now.

XXXI

Love of tropical plants. (If I knew their names I would write their poems.) My one frustrated ambition: to be a Latin professor. My second: to be a botanist. I angle them in.

XXXII

When I meet Mies van der Rohe, great in age, late in fame, I say to myself with smug sadness: a true artist, unconscious of people. (This was all false.)

XXXIII

The artist in the man or the man in the artist. Annihilation.

XXXIV

I have to play tricks on the avant-garde. That's what I'm here for. If I don't take the wrong side, who will?

XXXV

The blossom returns to the pear tree. It's a butterfly. It's a haiku. I don't think I buy that. I want a power saw for Christmas.

XXXVI

Sweet Melancholy, the poet's stock in trade, gives way to hilarity. After success self-pity is a bore. No more love-making. Only the mechanics.

XXXVII

And the guilt comes from the repression of instinct needs. And the repression is done by Conscience. And Conscience is another name for Mother. And the work of art approves of us, turning our rage to love.

XXXVIII

The ugliest theme set in the most exquisite stanzas. Rhyme
your insanity away. The poem is crazy-clean.

XXXIX

Rhyme or reason, you can't have both. Fiction or truth, you
can't have both. The vapors of the heart or the logic
of the case. The easel painting and the photo. Bird
song and phonograph record. The gaze swimming or
the eye on the object. The fast unto death or the finan-
cial report. The child on the swing or the man hanging
in space. Actual forgiveness or retribution. Involuntary
action or a matter of principle. Animal need and toilet
training. Poetry and civilization. The White Goddess
and the battle-ax. And form and content, and all
that.

XL

Prove you are less destructive than the poet. Prove that the
great slow prose-poem of the analysis does not lead to
the artificial paradise.

XLI

In the last days of Empire the Senate will try anything. Poets
arrive sheepishly on the platform under the mighty
seal. A display of abandoned clothing and loose hair.
Voices speaking as if through tubes. One of history's
regular truces with magic.

XLII

When the rage of the poem is oned with the fine forms; when
the bad feeling is oned with conscience: order, peace
and wholeness descend; we flow back into life. (Poetry
of the ill.)

XLIII

When we feel the natural streamings of life; when joy is its
own vector: when we shrug off the fine forms and the
lofty sayings and say with simplicity and power: I
pride myself on the general pleasure. Therefore I
praise. And what I hate, I hate with joy. (Poetry of
the hale and hearty.)

XLIV

One makes concessions. Times have changed. Now all things
are the measure of man, it's hard to find a decent god
or muse.

XLV

My friend, all men are creative. It's the natural state of affairs.
Paintings of children, quickly slain.

XLVI

The Finalists are upon us! Girls with golden crowns reading
The Queen of Queens. Throngs of virgins competing
for the coup de grâce. They sit on the backs of presi-
dents and caudillos, strumming their long-muscled
thighs. Whole nations are reduced to tears of achieve-
ment. Doctors march through the immense throngs
collecting their fees.

XLVII

You say "the institutions of the mind." That's poetry, too. You
say this tends toward wanted moral control. Have it
your way. Name the institutions of the peacock's mind.
Or the lowly chicken.

XLVIII

It all fits together, your logical poem. Art is happy medicine.
And so it is in your hospital.

III
End Paper

❡65

French poetry that always goes itself one better.

French poetry of figure 5's and rust carnations.

French poetry of the tongue that tastes of women and children, spatulas and rubber plants.

French poetry of the tiniest print to be read with bifocals when snow first enters the rain with its wicked announcements of defeat.

French poetry of marginal headaches, wood fires, cold, sixteen-millimeter surrealist films, Martinique jazz and the woman across the way, utmost gravity and indestructible balance, winner of the double medallion,

Easter Island images, the monstrous solemnity of patriotic children and ribbons.

French poetry of convenience, Satanism, baroque brass keys to hospitals, and cats.

French poetry of the line drawn with the fist on the pale nuance,

Overly cultivated snows, sick castles.

French poetry of the exquisite ruins of conversation.

French poetry that upsets the stomach of the future.

Of frockless priests, glorious geometricians, child insurrectionists.

French poetry of the Statue of Liberty, battered by kisses and dentists,

Ropy veins of the feet of matrons and whores, stigmata, épée.

French poetry of the Missouri River, the Platte, Yarra, gutter water of the rue Jacob.

Gloire, Vrai, et cetera.

¶66

What kind of notation is in my *Time* file for my life, especially my death? Will they say I died, O God? If they don't say I died how can I die? There it is fine and relevant to die, an honor so to speak, interesting as divorce.

What's in my file at the F.B.I.? What's my symbol when they flick me out? Am I a good American or a borderline case? Can I hold my liquor? Have I ever been cleared, and if so, of what?

Dear Fame, I meet you in the damnedest places. You smile, you walleyed bitch, but you look over my shoulder for a prearranged signal: something has come up on the other side of the room.

My life, my own, who is writing you on what pale punch cards? Deep-thinking machine, have you got my number?

A hundred oligarchs in identical suits are sitting around a table shaped like a uterus, alphabetizing greatness. I say to myself: all men are great. I would like to cry but have forgotten how. Now I remember: they used to come to me, those journalists with humble pencils. They begged me from their hats: say something big; give us an execution; make bad weather. I failed them badly. I couldn't grow a beard.

I guess I haven't built my ship of death. The word "image" is now in government. The doors are all closing by remote control. But when I meet the almighty Publicity Director, name-dropper of kings, I'll shake his hand and say: once I kissed Fame (mouth like an ass hole) but only for fun. He'll tear up the punch cards and think for a minute.

¶67

As you say (not without sadness), poets don't see, they feel. And that's why people who have turned to feelers seem like poets. Why children seem poetic. Why when the sap rises in the adolescent heart the young write poetry. Why great catastrophes are stated in verse. Why lunatics are named for the moon. Yet poetry isn't feeling with the hands. A poem is not a kiss. Poems are what ideas feel like. Ideas on Sunday, thoughts on vacation.

Poets don't see, they feel. They are conductors of the senses of men, as teachers and preachers are the insulators. The poets go up and feel the insulators. Now and again they feel the wrong thing and are thrown through a wall by a million-volt shock. All insulation makes the poet anxious: clothes, strait jackets, iambic five. He pulls at the seams like a boy whose trousers are cutting him in half. Poets think along the electric currents. The words are constantly not making sense when he reads. He flunks economics, logic, history. Then he describes what it feels like to flunk economics, logic, history. After that he feels better.

People say: it is sad to see a grown man feeling his way, sad to see a man so naked, desireless of any defenses. The people walk back into their boxes and triple-lock the doors. When their children begin to read poetry the parents watch them from the corner of their eye. It's only a phase, they aver. Parents like the word "aver" though they don't use it.

¶68

Randall, I like your poetry terribly, yet I'm afraid to say so. Not that my praise keeps you awake—though I'm afraid it does. I can't help liking them. I even like the whine, the make-believe whiplash with the actual wire in it. Once when you reviewed me badly (you must) I wrote you: "I felt as if I had been run over but not hurt." That made you laugh. I was happy. It wasn't much of a triumph but it worked. When people ask about you I am inclined to say: He's an assassin (a word I never use). I'm inclined to say: Why are you always yourself? Your love of Rilke—if it's love— your intimacy with German and God knows what all, your tenderness and terrorization, your prose sentences —like Bernini graves, staggeringly expensive, Italianate, warm, sentences once-and-for-all. And the verses you leave half-finished in mid-air—I once knew a woman who never finished a sentence. Your mind is always at its best, your craft the finest craft "money can buy" you would say with a barb. I'm afraid of you. Who wouldn't be. But I rush to read you, whatever you print. That's news.

❡69

They held a celebration for you, Charles, in Iowa. I was asked but I regretted. It was the hundredth birthday of your book, your proper Christian book called *Flowers of Evil*. (Or is it THE *Flowers of Evil*? I never know.) And in that hymnal, how well you made yourself in the image of Poe—Poe with a cross, that's what you are, adored of the gangster age. In fact, aren't you a children's poet? Aren't you the Lewis Carroll of small vice? Your shabby Wonderland of pus and giant nipple, your cats and jewels and cheap perfumes, your licking Lesbians and make-believe Black Mass,

O purulence of Original Sin. And always playing it safe in the end, like Disneyland. So many safety devices, pulleys, cranks, classical Alexandrines. It's Iowa for you, restless spirit, where elderly ladies embezzle millions in the *acute gratuite*. You'll need no naturalization papers here. And yet I loved you once, and Delacroix and Berlioz—all in my gangster age. The little boy in me loved you all, O solemn Charles, so photogenic. And this is my flower for your anniversary. I fashioned it of Mexican tin and black nail polish, little French Swinburne burning in Iowa City.

❡70

There is prayer in religion, and that is self-defeating. There is prayer outside religion; that is natural. It is the final intensity of wish. But to pray to a being outside yourself is only speaking the truth to yourself. If there is no other way to tell the truth, then pray. But don't expect any bargains. The Jain women kneel and chant before the marble idol with hideous eyes. The Catholic follows the plaster Virgin seated atop a motorcar. The old Jew beats his breast in atonement. These are paltry ways to tell the truth. No child would pray without being forced by fear. Prayer is a form of fear. Prayer is a way to make yourself hear. If all men knelt together over the earth and prayed with one mighty breath for the end of war they would still rise up with guns in their hands. For prayer is based on fear and not on love. If a man loves he throws away his weapons, and every weapon is a prayer. The brutal boxer crosses himself in the ring like an ape. The generals invoke

the blessings of God before the slaughter. The hunters
bless the hounds. In Siena they bring the race horse
to the altar; if he empties himself on the floor that
is good luck. Prayer is always against. Acts are the
only positive prayer. A book of prayers is a childish
machine for postponing acts of love and charity. To
the tree the woodsman should say: you are beautiful
but I must cut you down. I will use you well. Who
sees a soul imprisoned in a tree is a dangerous lunatic.
If prayer were for the feast of bodily love, it would
be good.

❡71

The teachers of culture hate science but the teachers of
science do not hate culture. The teachers of poetry
hate machines but the builders of machines give money
to poets. As priests lives in two worlds, the actual
world and the dim-lit world of their psychosis, so do
the teachers of arts. The teachers of arts live in the
church of the masterpiece and condemn all else. They
despise the farmer, the mechanic, the bacteriologist.
All this must be unlearned. The worshipers must be
cured to live in the world outside their arts. Only then
will the arts flow freely from all men to all men, as
the things of science flow in every direction over the
earth. For the arts carry the sickness of mind past.
The enslaved paintings repeat the feudal error. Pride
of nation leaps from pathological music, enshrining
murder, sanctifying death. We kill the living in the
child by our strong teaching. We kill with discipline
and commands. Till the child is freed in the world of the

school, the teaching of the things of man will continue to kill.

❡72

To make the child in your own image is a capital crime, for your image is not worth repeating. The child knows this and you know it. Consequently you hate each other. When the child hates the parent or the parent hates the child, both produce soldiers, quiet, beautifully dressed for the kill of "barbarians." The mother caresses the medals of her darling. The father salutes at Arlington Cemetery. The child is always lost in antique frustrations. On the child is poured the blood of churches. Babies are taught to salute the flag and to hate their sex. The suffix "hood" is made untouchable: motherhood, fatherhood, brotherhood, manhood, statehood.

A child is for love, for biologic power. A child is for play and admiration, laughter and terror. A child is for total concentration and absolute giving and absolute taking. A child demands and merits the collective affection of the universe. The child is lying in the egg of the rattlesnake or in the womb of Mozart's mother or the hating-house of Arthur Rimbaud or in the baby-green leaf of the rubber plant of the living room, but really in the child of love. The love of the child is pure destruction. Then let us be destroyed by this new beauty, who live in a time when we fight fire with fire and war with war and kill the little with the big—as if that were a solution even for the Department of Sanitation.

❡73

Each in her well-lighted picture window, reading a book or
  magazine, the Amsterdam whores look quite domestic.
  The canals, as picturesque as expected, add their
  serenity. The customers stroll from window to window,
  back and forth, comparing merchandise. Where a curtain is drawn, business is being transacted. These are
  big, fine, strapping whores, heavy in the leg, blond, as
  is the preference. They don't display their wares, no
  more than crossing a leg. It's like a picture gallery,
  Flemish School, silent through varnish and glaze.
  What detail, what realism of texture, what narrative!
  And look at this masterpiece:

A solid blond sits in her window at an angle. She appears to
  be looking out, expressionless. Just back of her stands
  an African king in round white hat and lengthy white
  embroidered robe of satin, it may be. Behind him
  stands his servant, very straight. The king's face is a
  thin and noble ebony. And without looking at either
  African the whore holds one hand back of her shoulder,
  feeling the robe of the African king with eloquent
  fingers, weighing the heft of the silk in her thoughtful
  hand.

❡74

The prophets say to Know Thyself: I say it can't be done. It
  takes many to know the one self and you are only one
  of the many who know yourself. Man is mostly involuntary. Consciousness is only a tiny part of us.

As dreams protect the sleeper, so does the waking memory keep your pain. A man who knows himself too well falls ill. Self-knowledge is a dangerous thing, tending to make man shallow or insane. Those poets who study their own consciousness are their own monsters. Each look in the mirror shows a different self. You are not one but many yous. These many yous the feudalists of thought call soul. They would make you a slave to your dead selves; they will not let you walk away into the freedom of yourself becoming. The coral animal turns to jagged stone after it dies; the dead selves build into an underwater cathedral, housing for brilliant and deadly jaws. Know not Thyself. No two days are ever the same in the world; and no two days of the self are ever the same. All spirals outward, large or microscopic. Creation renewing itself forever does not look back. Look back and turn to rock. The shell-shocked man is sleeping peacefully. I pray that when he wakes he will be himself again. But he wakes only into his shock. Somewhere in battle he saw himself and died. The lost ones return to some old self and sit there in the corner, laughing or crying.

¶75

I drove three thousand miles to ask a question. No answer, naturally. It served me right; I'm not the pilgrim type. I wanted a first-hand account of *him*: when he was alive, before they murdered him. When you worked with him, before they drove him insane, I laughed like the others. I said: My friend, you swim among the blues of the lunatic fringe as always. This is only another of your voyages. But did you leave him before he died or after? Did you go to the trial? Were you there when the police smashed the equipment? Did you visit him in the sunset of his mind?

In the soft San Diego sunset you turned your back. I don't want to talk about that, you said. Your little dogs leaped up at me with teeth. Our children ran wild together. Your wife sang beautifully. In the morning you cashed me a check, arriving at the bank in a foreign car.

Did you really recover from the death of your father? I must hear about the other from someone I know as well as you. You are the only one. We didn't get along was all you said. I don't want to discuss him. The disciples are scattered. They are all in hiding. It's against the law to post his books. Everyone seems ashamed for a different reason. Is his wife living, his child? Where is truth's underground? How long does love stay murdered? Did he have to sentence himself? The lab experiment of his life is proved—there must have been another way. Pictures that he took when the bulbs popped, each brighter than a thousand suns; the spiral poems he wrote under the electronic microscope—mad scientist, good German—fixed in my mind and locked in yours.

❡76

The day you discover that your favorite poet is a homosexual, and the heated argument dies down after an hour, and you have lost, you are like a prince who has been

brought bad tidings and you sit with an empty belly
while they take the messenger out of the room to be
shot. Tomorrow it will be different but tonight you feel
an impersonal sorrow as nagging as envy. When later
you read his poems, with another dimension added to
their music, they will seem more distant, like fine
translations. A dry wash of the face will suffice for
your pleasure. It's not the same as with Shakespeare
or the plain Cavafy. You can shrug at the Greeks and
the Bulgarians. But this is a secret that had to be
told to be known.

Close the door of your mind on those love letters. Beware of
the poison of pronouns. Suddenly you are coarse with
limitation, gruff before flowers, your own poems lumpy,
indelicate. The it-ness of trees! And Emily too? And
the brotherhood of man—is that one? Penitentiaries,
navies, hospitals, football teams! Where will it end?

Poet who lies with the sea, dancer who shrugs one shoulder,
lecturer with the turquoise ring, exquisite conversa-
tionalist, you with the beard and the lake-water eyes,
woman with the voice of woodwinds—why do you
slap me? Is there a poetry where what happens in
bed is lucky on the page and the poem is actually for
her?

❡77

Why am I happy writing this textbook? What sublime idiocy!
What a waste of time! A textbook on prosody at that.
Yet when I sit down to comb the business out, when I
address the easel of this task, I burn with an even

flame, I'm cooking with gas. There are some things so dull they hypnotize like the pendulum of a clock; so clockwork and quotidian they make the flesh delirious like fresh water. X-ray the poem, give it a thorough physical, a clean bill of health. We can see everything but the flow of blood. What Latin and Greek nomenclature! But this is order, order made to order. This is system to plot and plan. This is definition, edges clean as razors. Simplification, boldface, indented. I know there is no such thing as a textbook. I know that all textbooks are sold the second the course is over. I know that a book sold is a dead book. And I dream, like others, of writing a textbook that is not a textbook, a book that not even a student would part with, a book that makes even prosody breathe. So, when the sun shines with the nine o'clock brightness and the coffee swims in my throat and the smoke floats over the page like the smoke of a ship's funnel, then I romanticize. I make a muse of prosody, old hag. She's just a registered nurse, I know, I know, but I have her sashay, grind and bump, register Alcaics, Sapphics, choriambs (my predilection). She's trained all right. She's second nature herself. She knows her job, I mine. We'll work it out: it may be poetry. Blueprints are blue. They have their dreams.

¶78

They erect a bust of me after my death. I know the right alcove, where the students sit, in the library corridor, smoking and joking about the professors. "I fought with tooth and nail to save my niche."

A bust in the modern mode, more than slightly abstract, in a dull metal perhaps, of the new alloys I love. No lapis lazuli "big as a Jew's head cut off at the nape." I wish I had a leonine head, the kind to start a sculptor's fingers twitching.

There was a bust of me a student made, life-size and a good likeness, age twenty-one when I wore a pompadour. In plaster it was much too white. We painted it green, then pink, then black, then sandpapered it down and called it Scrofula. One night we stuck it in a mound of dirt outside where they were mending the street. That was the end of it. Baltimore has too many monuments already.

Baltimore has Poe and also Lanier. Lizette Reese and Francis Scott Key. Baltimore has poets and poets. —Which uncle put the money up?

❡79

Posterity is a literary racket. Posterity is a switchboard to past, present, and future. Posterity is an intercom system devised by the brain of super-educationalists in faraway almost nonexistent places like offices. Posterity lives in the vaults of the nearest insurance company. Posterity is for the fabulously rich. The poor plant potatoes in the bathtub and dandle their children and listen to beery poetry on broken sofas.

The term *generation* is a deadly weapon. When a poet says "my generation," move off a few feet. He probably has a switch-blade knife up his sleeve, and it's for "my" generation. If you want to join the poet's army, just give the password: my generation. Generations are organizations, like General Motors. Posterity is a de facto government of clean-jawed men with high ideals and two telephones in every bathroom. It's always the generation that takes the credit for whatever is credited. Always posterity that catches the hell of the last generation. Posterity lies in wait for the innocent, a monstrous grave to swallow the grandchildren, dug by the lean-jawed voices of ideals. A source close to posterity tells me that this generation isn't going well and may have to take its place in the catacombs.

¶80

The Jesuit father said to me: Before you meet your poetry class there are two things we wish to know. Do you believe in Original Sin and Freedom of the Will? I faltered in the Patmore light and said: As far as I know. —And that was that. I got the job. I might have gotten it anyway, as far as I know.

At the cocktail party I asked the rabbi: Do Jews believe in Original Sin? The Talmud of his mind flew open like a gate. I followed him through twisting streets, lost him in shadow and dropped into a tavern. His answer was No, as far as I could tell.

As for myself, the answer is No. I lied to the father and myself.

Freedom of the Will sounds good, if you don't know what it means. It sounds democratic, in a manner of speaking. But it's the ultimate bait for the faithful fish. It means the contradiction of the cause. It means

you can swoon at the impossible. It means Giordano
dying at the stake. It means the big white lie of Galileo.
It means the double standard of the truth: the daily
truth and the Sunday truth. It means morality for
children in diapers; chaplains in uniform.

❡81

God couldn't stand the sight of Cain. Nor could he stand the
flowing rows of wheat and the sweet rye grass as green
as a garden. The smoke flew back in the face of Cain
and choked him. Abel wept. Abel was afraid of his
brother and went for a walk in the open country. The
jealousy of God sat heavily on Cain. He killed his
younger brother with a stone. It might have been
worse, much worse. Then Cain's own children, forbid-
den their land, invented cities and the culture of cities.
But God hated cities as fast as they were built. And the
cities were never really on His side. The cities grew
bigger, the women more beautiful, and God more
angry.

❡82

The fish are exempt for some reason. The waters of the
abyss wash everything clean. Now the animals are
scampering down the mountainside headed for the
swimming jungles. The patriarch and his family move
in awe on the mountain, under the sky of broken

clouds where the sun pours through and the rainbow bends its colors. They sing, they pray like pilgrims from over the sea. God has regained his temper. The murders of Cain and Lamech are over and done with. But shortly Noah harvests the grapes and gets thoroughly drunk. Lying nude and erect on his bed he is found by his son. This constitutes a crime and the son is cursed forever. It's the ritual of shame enforced by God. The patriarch destroys the son because of his own unconscious natural lust. (The other brothers backed into the tent, so as not to see the holy object, and covered it with a blanket. For which they were richly rewarded.)

¶83

What the analyst said when he came from the exhibit (he was rather drunk) amounted to this: A clean white wall in an uncluttered room is the ground. You take a clean white wall and hang a rock, a sock, a split of log, a bag of dreck—give it the frame of a clean white wall, and that's abstract.

I looked around the clean white room. Schwitters fritterings of old bus tickets, gracefully mounted bit on bit, for fade of color, take of depth, alone on its panel. Bronze drip of narrow stems of bronze Giocometti; teakwood base. Enormous almost idiot head of Christ, hydrocephalic, brushed in dusty yellows. A female thigh, reddish close-grained jarrah wood, with a high polish.

I love abandoned barns weathered to silver, the drip of rust from reinforcement iron stars on old American brick;

driftwood of course; objects found to hand; fondling-stones; packets of Japanese black pebbles; shards; un-dressed planking; ax marks on a fashionable mantle, twelve by twelve; pock-marked travertine; rose-red hinges; ten-cent-store utensils; comic strips with paren-theses denoting frustration or beating wings; Samuel Greenberg and Rupert Brooke.

¶84

The preacher (say Episcopal) alone on a lone day (Tuesday perhaps, off season for great holidays) in his fine small church (not small if you are in it long enough), really in solitude in the minor splendor. One supposes he has finished his chores, whatever they are, and is returning the absorption of the stage-lit solitude. Nevertheless everything is present, with objects having taken on the quality of human beings. He's not what you would call a contemplative. He snatches time like a schoolteacher, or waits for it, miserly, knowing that it will come with interest. And when it comes (which is rather more often than anyone expects, or even wants), his first sensation is collapse, his second to sit where the Sunday people pray. There, though it has the musk of a railroad station (not really), he takes a seat for a moment, gets up, sits down. He is one of them now, in the back of his head. The hedges are such a brown that spring is about to thorn on the world-side of the purple glass with its legends so strictly ruled on the calendar. He has no grief. This paperwork of saving souls! Could there be quiet in the stolen moment, moment of fame with God. But everything stirs, even though noiselessly. Could there be thoughts that turn to stone after the hammering, forever. O leaves of stone, come forth in a cool summering of prayer and change my spirit into a fine small church on the world's quietest street. My hands of vellum folded, I could pray.

¶85

I'm writing this poem for someone to see when I'm not looking. This is an open book. I want to be careful to startle you gently. The poem is about your looking at it, as one looks at a woman covertly. (I wonder what she's doing in this town; it's a long way from the look in her eyes.) The rings of my big notebook stand open like the rib cage of a baracuda. Careful with your fingers.

I'm writing this poem for an after-dinner friend who's using my pipe tobacco or my pen. I'd like some phrase to catch his eye. I'd like some phrase to wake him up in the early hours, as one wakes up with a fragment of tune in his head (the melody for the day). The toilet bowls glow graciously and there's a box of the best Kleenex on the sink. I'm writing this poem for hospitality. I can't stand people who say Help Yourself. That always means Don't Be a Pig. Tired of picking the locks of poems I leave this one for all and sundry. To put your name in it would be a dirty trick.

Younger I dreamed of being a poet whose trash basket was rifled by scholars. I learned to write trash-basket poems. But this is closer to my real desire. I'm writing this poem as much for you as a poem is possible. It stands there like a half-filled glass, both coming and going. I'm a bad host. The drinks are too strong; I don't know how to carve (I say with a grin, I'm left-handed). This is a poem to sneak at a glance. (I'm writing it to mean, not be.)

¶86

In a flash I see my mistake and put it out of my mind. But I'm through tearing out my marginalia, erasing my notes and drunken commentaries. "The man writes prose like a lunatic." By the time I run across this again I am praising his prose and getting it published. Here's an old poem that loves Eliot. I outline the Zohar, especially the glyph of the Tree of Life. It's a long way around to the truth that you started with. Belief is the greatest tragedy of man. Only the heroes walk through life not even aware of belief. Lunatics! Saints!

When Tertullian died the angels jumped out of their nightgowns and went at it like goats. Any belief, the more far-fetched the better, can explain everything. It is diseased to believe. Now it's old Tolstoy who has me by the short hairs and hisses *hate Shakespeare*. I hate him for a lecture or two. Then I hate Leo. Then I'm back to normal. As for the errors, think nothing of them. Somebody fools you every day of your life. Track down the jokers and nail them flat. Never mind backtracks. Don't look behind you. And if anybody asks you: never apologize, even to God.

⟪87

Cat called me a Jewish pig. Cat said to me in a voice so normal she might be ordering ham from a yard-high menu: You are the most insensitive man I've ever met.

Cat and I were walking down the Cathouse street off Bughouse Square in Chicago. Her husband was trying to lose us (you can hardly blame him). Where is your lovely husband, Cat? She wheeled around and pointed through the neon baleful glare: There comes the little fucker, that little black thing two inches high.

She sulked on a sofa in a shabby dress, looking like an Irish maid on her day off in the walnut-paneled living room. She seethed with worms at so much rich stupidity. Hell flowed from her mouth like streams of horse, splashing the blue Picassos.

For breakfast we have beer. Where the scum of fame backed up in the estuary Cat bathed with hopeless soap. The sky grew dingier than pans. In the vomit of news she spun like a carousel and fell through sobs to the dromedary dolls.

Cat went walking through the slaughterhouse where the prime hogs dance on the end of a chain and the throats are slit to empty the black blood. She groaned in the screaming of pork and was given perfume.

Cat left her laundry and forgot to get it. Five miles in the air you could hear her scream of love. At the soup kitchen of poets she gloomed like a sphinx. She stroked the oxygen tank like a bomb with a name. She exhausted the language of blame. With the dry shrapnel of love

she shaved her head in the gleaming sleet of literature.
Her typewriter keys were tipped with tetanus praise.
She cursed the cyclamen, good Saint Cat.

¶88

He said it: Kill the poet in yourself. He said it well. Now he
is surrounded by juries in every direction. Whole
passages are read by the court clerk; the women bow
their heads as if in prayer. Some have never even heard
the words that kill. The men are always angriest or
aggrieved. I think: the pig is taboo to the Jews because
it was once their god. Are those words gods? The
people want their poetry of not saying, don't touch,
hold your shoulders straight. They turn the book in
their hands like a time bomb. Something goes off in
their laps but no one is frightened. Much talk of taking
a bath. A bidet is brought for exhibit. Demonstrations.
Laughter. Waving of state flags. No one is certain
precisely what the issue is. The testimony grows
learned; big words are rolled in like balls of dung.
Why are the edges of the Bible red not blue? I think
we are losing. The experts falter. Housewives examine
their fingernails: this is the end. The hilarious thing is
the way he sides with the judges, like Jesus. The veil is
rent by a tremendous blot. Dogs cry in their sleep.
Children playing doctor are hustled off to the federal
prisons. The wife of the President crosses herself before releasing the bottle of champagne against the lead
wall of the fall-out shelter. The judge is clutching the
Good. Nobody knows what happened to the True. The

Beautiful has fainted dead away (she has her instructions).

¶89

Dylan wasn't dapper. Uncle Saul was a dandy. Dylan stole and borrowed. Uncle Saul likewise. Dylan stole a shirt or two and some bottles of whiskey. Uncle Saul purloined whole wardrobes, used checking accounts that didn't belong to him, charged at the best shops under others' names. Dylan wore motley, Uncle Saul silk. Dylan was short and curly. Uncle Saul wore Cuban heels to raise himself and ordered Scotch in the barber's chair. Dylan played at pinballs. Uncle won the monthly rent at poker or bridge. Dylan borrowed women. Uncle Saul hired them and kept them in love nests. Dylan's look was straight and far into your eyes. The eyes of Uncle Saul were always merry and shrewd but you couldn't see beyond their twinkle and scheme. Dylan was a civilian. Uncle wangled a commission in the Army, only to be discharged for juggling money records. Uncle Saul kept the table choking with laughter and sang falsetto and clowned in a lavender dressing gown, with masses of hair on his chest. Dylan toured America like a favorite nephew, sprinkling dynamite on the nipples of female professors. He had the discipline of a lovely knave.

Now both are dead, Dylan and Uncle Saul. Dylan was taken by the pickling of his beautiful brain. The sacred oxygen could not reach the convolutions. Uncle Saul was taken thrice by the heart, thrice by the broken personality. Uncle Saul joked in the lobby of the plush nuthouse, wearing a brilliant sportcoat and shined elegant shoes. The black hair dye had vanished; his hair was snowy white. They gave him the shock treatment until his heart exploded. Dylan lay inert with the Moses bumps on his forehead amidst the screaming of wives and the groans of lovers and drinkers. And the Beat said—iambic killed him.

⟨90

As busy ants tote bales of bread a dozen times their busy bulk, so you pack those compound words, your poems a freight train with a hundred cars, loaded with such technology as flattop fleets are made on. Jouncy rhythms, fiery flints, and you poke well with your pointy stick, neatly messing in the cuesta flesh of animals dead, the grosgrain swollen belly of the cat. Once I laughed at soggy verse. Not any more. You understand the talking machine called man.

You're a lady, you're a girl, and life under the wallpaper keeps you awake. It keeps me awake, the terror of the tiny teeth. Now day and night have interchanged. Day and night have traded sweaters, senseless as high-school girls or keepsake wives. Wrist watches run just when they feel like it. The old fish with a charm-bracelet lower lip comes up for air, goes down to think. The nightmare kicks like a foetus. All things have eyes, are watching each other, and death is only a broken promise. Under the comforter of earth, less safety. The smoke pays no attention to the wind. You're painting in blinding light with lots of darks. A boy rolling a hoop is running from something. You say all this as if you were the hostess.

❡91

Glottal as a bottle, everybody loves you, only you don't believe
it. Hulk of greenery among the desert great, your roots
grab continents of sham and groan. You masticate all
dictionaries and spew out one-word spitballs on the
walls. You blackboard buccaneers of blah. You housel
planetaria of spurt. You shoeshine flesh with hail and
hurt. Psychologically, you sport.

The music flutes: you're nursing Mother Goose. You know
her nasty secrets like a name (dirty old woman stink-
ing of gin). Have you found the pickled foetuses! Does
your poem purl in Polish? Who's bigger than you—
those squishy dreams?

The decencies file in: such pretty girls, such beardy boys.
Your rhythms that throb like ocean motors.

Now and then the darkness of stanzas. That ridge of ice-
capped sawtooth monuments bites at the sky like
industrial diamonds. You grit your teeth on broken
glass, sing with a geographical tongue on the sly nights
of Seattle. Art is a blood pudding foreign as frescoes.
Where you dig down we are, we are. Under the smoky
glass we are. How the flukes splash, ha-ha, baby!

❡92

When they ask about your poems I say: He writes like a truck
driver (if only you did). Your idiom coarse as Indian
hair, you click along on Union Pacific meters. You tell
your rhymes like beads; you ambiguate as well as the

gobbledegooks. Honor bright. We all came out of the
same army and joined the same generation of silence.
Each took the territory of his choice (yours is the
biggest). You handle Dante like a Cadillac. (Our
colleague drives a Mercedes-Rilke. Our serious one
can't tell the names of cars.) Good social conscience,
lover of gab and gag, you're known in every dimension,
heart like a halfback—

One time you beaned the lady-poet, I scratched my head.
What the hell were you trying to do? People attack
affinities. The gurus call you middlebrow; you shrug it
off. You feel at home in the poetry lab, a manual or two
under your belt. This isn't an ad or a tax return. It's a
Chanukah card with Haitian angels. The Christmas
seal says Help Fight Gongorism. You weave across the
country like a trend. Have you lost the essential bum?
It's not what you sit on. The busted image has melted
back together, as hot as cooling glass. Now that the
Bishop's got his ashes hauled.

❨93

As richly documented as the hell of priests, yes, there is a
hell, the hell of sick poets, the hell of history. Those in
whom honesty has turned to policy. Those diseased by
notice. Those who invent new prosodies, with a logical
or graphic notation. Those who wear the cold hand-
cuffs of rhyme. Those who construct a religion of the
beautiful, with symbols as the means and myth as the
end. Those who mistake rage for intensity, symmetry
for design, metaphor for focus, drunkenness for vision.
Those who make an example of their lives and who

commit acts of personal violence for public response. These inhabit the hell of poets.

Some die early by disease or accident. Some jump in the sea or drink lacerating poisons manufactured for toilets. Some lie in asylums with eyeballs metamorphosed to marble. (You cannot penetrate below their surface.) Some fall on their knees before two pieces of wood or a stone belly. Some join the revolutions and are gladly shot. Some become officials, laureates, men of affairs or major diplomats. Some become abstractionists, actuaries, mathematicians. Some become salesmen or lay priests, after their voluptuous poems are in print. Some become preachers in the last half of their lives, constructing faultless sermons. Some succumb to pageantry, some to algolagnia.

❡94

We pick some unsuspecting soul, usually a friend, on whom to visit a lifetime of frustration. Usually a friend, at one fell swoop. That's what friends are for.

Incapable of loyalty, I marvel at it, imitate it nicely. But the feeling comes from outside. It doesn't sprout in my own soil. I carry it from a florist of sorts, some man or woman of character, and tend it lovingly. It struggles manfully in my slant sun, flourishes in the room where I am. I scat the cat away with a loud newspaper. All my plants are exotics, bamboo, rubber, cocoa, some with names I have never found out. They do well in the hothouse of my eye; they bring admiring glances. I sketch the shadows now and then.

At the bottom of the rubber plant one great leaf is dying an
    interesting death. It dies with astonishing rapidity.
    Monday, a few dabs of bright yellow. Tuesday, a
    ladder of yellow on one side. Wednesday, half green,
    half yellow, split down the middle. Thursday a spot
    of deadly brown. Then the whole thing twists to a
    Dead Sea Scroll of deadness. A single new leaf will
    take a month to come.

What you say is true: I have no friends.

❦95

In the Clearing I am at peace. Place without memory or
    charm. Stores practically empty of goods, schools
    kindly and frightened. This Clearing is a beach with-
    out a sea.

Here there is only sporadic and symbolic violence. The clouds
    are all the news. Each tree is grown by hand.

By degrees, those who have ambience are alienated from the
    Dark Towers: the German groaning for the picture
    galleries; the bank director who bakes his own bread;
    the housewife with a flair for words who has given up
    bathing; the itinerant pianist with ice-blue eyes; the
    Siberian physicist with his smug compliments; the Ox-
    ford don with the dirtiest stories; the rabbi with the
    mystique of the Sabbath Queen; the bearded classicist
    with broken arches; the veteran bomber of three world
    wars. I talk to the man who brings the firewood. He
    gives me a wedge for a present.

The citizens of Nowhere scatter in all directions.

Upon my discharge from the Army my handwriting changed.
Neat slant characters gave way to square and upright.
The color of the ink no longer mattered. I met a poet
who printed all his words. (I thought this dangerous.)
I find I can barely read the mail that comes. Sometimes
I have it read to me. I tend to misunderstand the words.
My answers are brief. I still wait for the mailman, a
vestigial pleasure. Mail in the Clearing is lighter.

¶96

Balcony Scene

You have beautiful Middle Western legs.

Widow-woman, why on Memorial Day, you who love white,
did your bathing suit turn black? Woman in naked
white and black. He dove down the billion-dollar plane,
hands at the juke-box switches. The Christmas tree
was clicking in the window. Grief I never heard. Your
children walk on the soft excellent grass. Peonies lean
their hairdos fatly, hands on hips.

Fatlady, I love your face, sort of slapped together. And when
you walk (white bathing suit, black) it's as if one hip,
the right, for instance, were going out of joint, but to
return, a throwing motion, throwing-away, a gener-
osity. You bend from the vertical, raising your bottom
to the blazing sky.

Sunburn. Happy the widow with a hard white ass and a
willow tree. O pickpock moon, subject of all lost
poems, birthplace of tides et cetera, true bottom of the
sea et cetera, O wallsocket.

Vacation

Goldness and whiteness of woman, like a Grand Rapids bed
or a Sunday paper of brides. The bride coated with
power stands in the strongest light at last. She is clean.
—The sculptor sets his jaw and drives to the junk yard.
There he can breathe.

Love on the deathbed, love deeper than sunset. The Bros.
are coming. What! is it nothing but that? Is love
nothing but that? Battle of Waterloo, nothing but that?
Fraulein, allumeuse? Or to end a sentence with a prep-
osition?

Six cases of bourbon returned to the caterer and the flowers
divided. Hymen hymenaee.

Man with the lamp, hands of ferroconcrete, vellum of hand,
the skin as soft as kid. Big black flashlight, size of a
horsecock, mother's gift. Night silent as handwriting,
night with two cats on long thin ropes. The leather coat
of early night on the great wet lakes. Woman, homo
normalis!

Consider also their baths, their bows, their brown blood, their
pots, their stenches, out of which the greatest of
sonnet cycles.

Anti-Poem

Orchards hang in the newspaper of sky. It's snowing names
and addresses over the world, O lovely splash!

In dry percussion, hammers of prosperity practice against the
too-green corn. The wheat field narrows, then dis-
appears, leaving a memory of dry wind-waves. Who
eats dry wheat but boys, wheat the hue of the backs of

eighteen-century books. Children spring from the doors
where there are no trees. Roofer up there, it's been a
good day.

On the oldest plains rise the newest houses, smelling of rose
sawdust and nails. The clammy mortar structures itself. Everyone looks like a possible Survivor. Is he one?
Is she one? Who reinvented the secret stairway, pas-
sage to the room of Poe, chapel without a god?

Christ is in voice. The mayor is pleased with the murals. The
Jews next door are less noisy. Set the alarm for seven.

The child says: You have gray hair—you are an idiot!

The beauty is gone across the fence, the busted nose in poetry.

When I see you walk away, I love you.

When I see your back, the curves of your shoulders, your hair
the world worked on.

When I see you holding ginger by the throat.

The way a woman takes—anything (but never refuses)—is
beautiful, so to speak. The way she turns it in her
hands, holding it, not holding it. The way it catches
the light and she appraises it (in the pawnshop of her
mind). Magnetism enters the thing, five minutes, eight
minutes, zero minutes. She'll throw it in the trash or
give it to someone she's better than. The gestures of
those handsome hands.

Death of a Student

Down the funeral aisle ("my" student in coffin, car wreck,
youngish death, eyeglasses polished, suit pressed as if
for class, except that he's dead) come the grandparents,
farmers, barely walking. Followed by yet another

generation—over the arm of a younging man a girl about three asleep—drugged?—her golden pony tail flopping, asleep.

Tie tied, suit without lint, the curt sadistic sermon. Love stiffens her back. The child evades the question, as if tossing her hair. Nihilo lies sleeping.

Basement Apartment

Hymen's got a cold. Hymen, your nose is running.

My love, you look like Beethoven, like you were hit by a truck.

You look like a fucking skull.

It's six o'clock, you're drunk, you speak Greek in your sleep, you snore like Henry the Ninth. Wake up and take the dimes off my eyes.

The head of shame is red. The revenue stamp on the liquor bottle is red. Accidental baby, where's the Med School?

Trafe is the color of my true love's hair. Thank God for rain, blizzards, onions, and clap. Head like a broken sunflower rolling on its neck.

Coat, I place my hands in your empty pockets, thievery of nihilo, all the same illegal. Hands are illegal, teeth and tongue, books, bottles, dry rust carnations, babies, weeping, and law.

Two cars, one male, one female in every nest of love.

Two hearts with internal combustion engines.

Two broomsticks in every garage—ride 'em cowboy!

Bird's nest for a birthday or a sword.

Wholicity! Verset.

The Witches Are Flying

I know a man who bought a fire engine to rebuild into a twice-life-size Stutz Bearcat. There's a man in New York builds cars a hundred feet long so they can't turn corners.

Big sonnet. Thing without eyes; that moves. Verset.

Letters stuck with dirt as a signature. Verset.
Byzant! Byzant! Stutz Bearcat long as a block. Glory, glory, glory, packaged or loose, or in throwaway bottles. Duende the darkness.

Autumn, a generation of trees gives up the ghost. Hour of football, bituminous butterflies, vicious professors varnishing their desks.

Autumn, some prisoner in Iowa gives up the ghost. In bad faith I pretend to hear the creaking of his rope in the sole moment before his neck cracks—who has just eaten two helpings of shortcake and asked the newspapers for our forgiveness.

Third ejaculation of the hanged man, last seed spent in the hand of justice. Sixty-five poets cower in the poetry shack expecting advancement.

Teamsters Union

Sorrow has moved away like happiness. The Bros. depart.

When poetry is written the trucks come. The Bros. are here. China is being packed in Cheerio cartons, the best books are wrapped in Dacron drawers. The Bros. are careful.

Great vans that smash vacationers like cockroaches, vans with names as high as windmills, noble, impersonal.

End in sight, I have your phone number. I make the nasty clicks of the dial, quickly, with the accuracy of the drum of an empty revolver. Sounds fall, like when the pussy willow goes to seed, or heady dandelions or sycamore trash balls.

Ex stasis—out of this world. Teamsters Union.

The song of the phone has quit. To kalon, to kakon.

The clock-radio is still, la mauvoise foi. What! Is it nothing but that?

Night. The sky is torn and ripped, creating panic in the eye of the beholder. Few look up. The van sits in the duende darkness with the admirable stupidity of officials.

And sleeping beauty Nihilo lies sleeping.

The Bros. depart, the pride of ownership dismantled, pieces to be salvaged in a distant state, checkbook with its pink tongue hanging out.

Sorrow like distant thunder. Brilliant and big on distant O Street the Bros. pass by. O Street that cuts the town in half like a pie, woman sawn in the middle. Middle street of mental merchandise and distant crags.

Sun goes to the end of the road with immense self-pity. Rises the same on the opposite side, catatonic in beauty, showered with glory and dimes.

Love is the exact reverse of desire. O. In the act of love the person goes out of himself. O. It goes forth toward the object; it is continuous; it is fluid. O.

Delacroix: I write to Mlle. de Forget.

Daughter: Kitty, you bust my masterpiece!

ABOUT THE AUTHOR

KARL SHAPIRO was born in Baltimore, Maryland, on November 10, 1913, and attended the University of Virginia and Johns Hopkins University. In 1946 he was appointed Consultant in Poetry at the Library of Congress, and then, in 1947, he joined the faculty of Johns Hopkins University, where he taught writing courses. In 1950 he became editor of *Poetry: A Magazine of Verse*. Mr. Shapiro is now Professor of English at the University of Nebraska, where he was until recently editor of *Prairie Schooner*. He is a member of the National Institute of Arts and Letters.

Mr. Shapiro's poems, essays and reviews have appeared in leading literary magazines. His second volume of verse, *V-Letter and Other Poems*, was awarded the Pulitzer Prize in 1945.